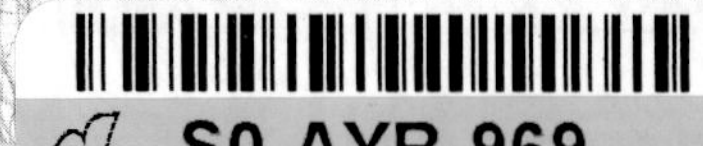

Three Shadows

Cyril Pedrosa

Translated by Edward Gauvin

First Second
NEW YORK & LONDON

You're thirteen weeks old.
Cold shock, as never wished before:

to die and be buried, close
under the packed earth,

safe for an eternal instant
from my constant, fevered fear that

you'd die. Relief
warming my veins,

and you relieved forever
of my looming, teary watch.

– Deborah Garrison, *Not Pleasant But True*

Back then...
CHUK
CHUK
CHUK
...Life was simple and sweet.

Everything was
simple and sweet...

The taste of cherries, the cool shade, the fresh smell of the river...

That was how we lived, in a vale among the hills...
...sheltered from storms...

Ignorant of the world,
as though on an island...
...Peaceful and
untroubled.

And then...
...Then everything changed.

crick
crackle
M-mm-
mommy?
The Art of Stew
Joachim?
What are you doing up?
Go!
Back to bed with you!
Mommy-
I'm scared of the shadows.

puff
puff
puff
Well.
Theeere now...
Come here, sweetie!
Let's get you to bed.
Obviously your daddy's far too busy to tuck you in.
Okay.
Well, he did say "Mommy" I'm scared of the shadows!
Ha Ha Ha

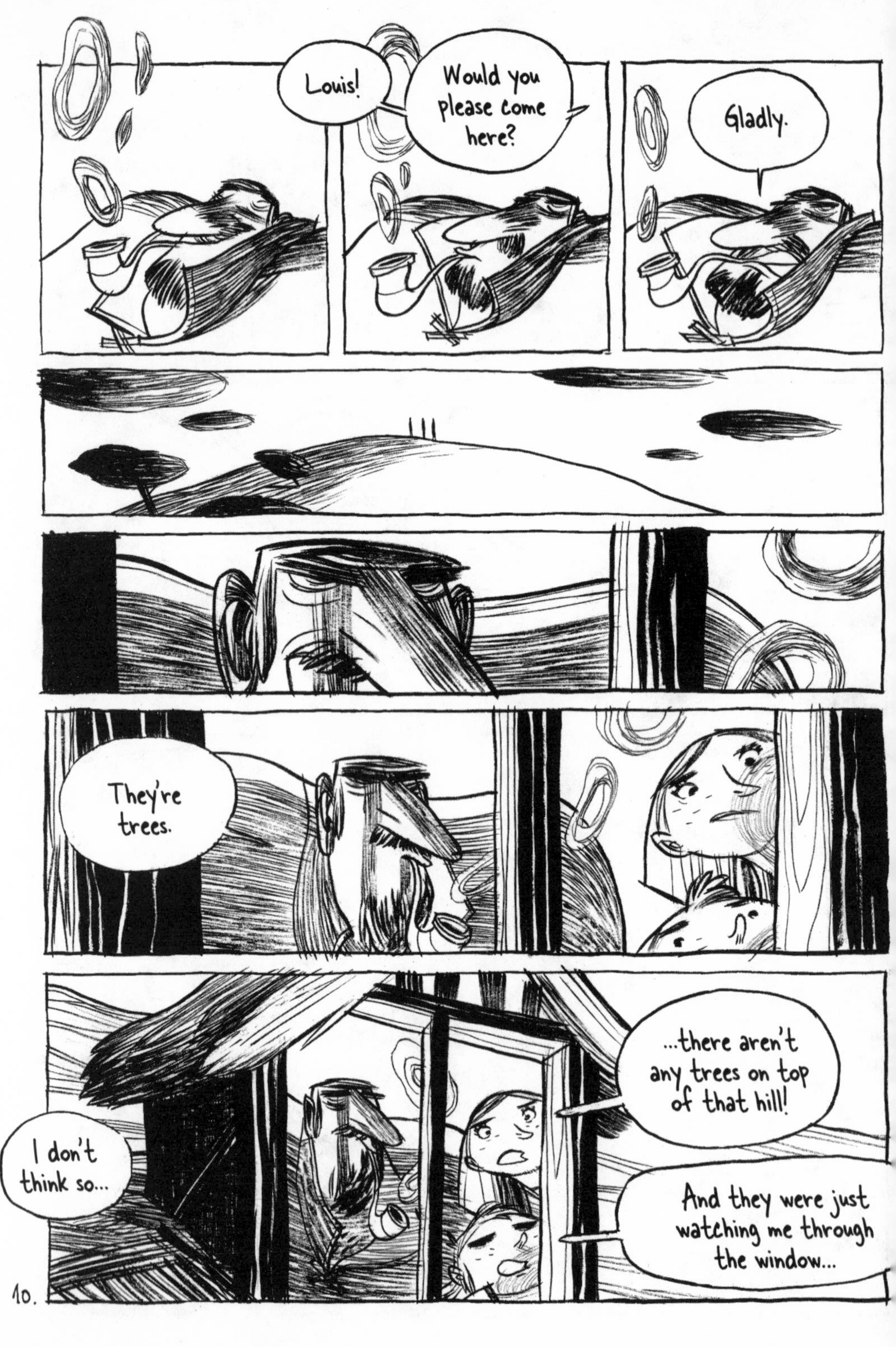
Louis!
Would you please come here?
Gladly.
They're trees.
...there aren't any trees on top of that hill!
I don't think so...
And they were just watching me through the window...

You must've been having a nightmare.
It's nothing.
Clearly, they're...
trees.
They—
They're moving!
Okay then!
So there are horsemen on the hill!
So what??
Daddy...
...I'm scared of horsemen.

All the same...
it's rather strange...
Are you two finished yet?
Really!!
Some travelers pass by on the hill...
...while we're safe and snug at home!
I don't see what's so...
"strange"!
Well.
Back to bed, then?

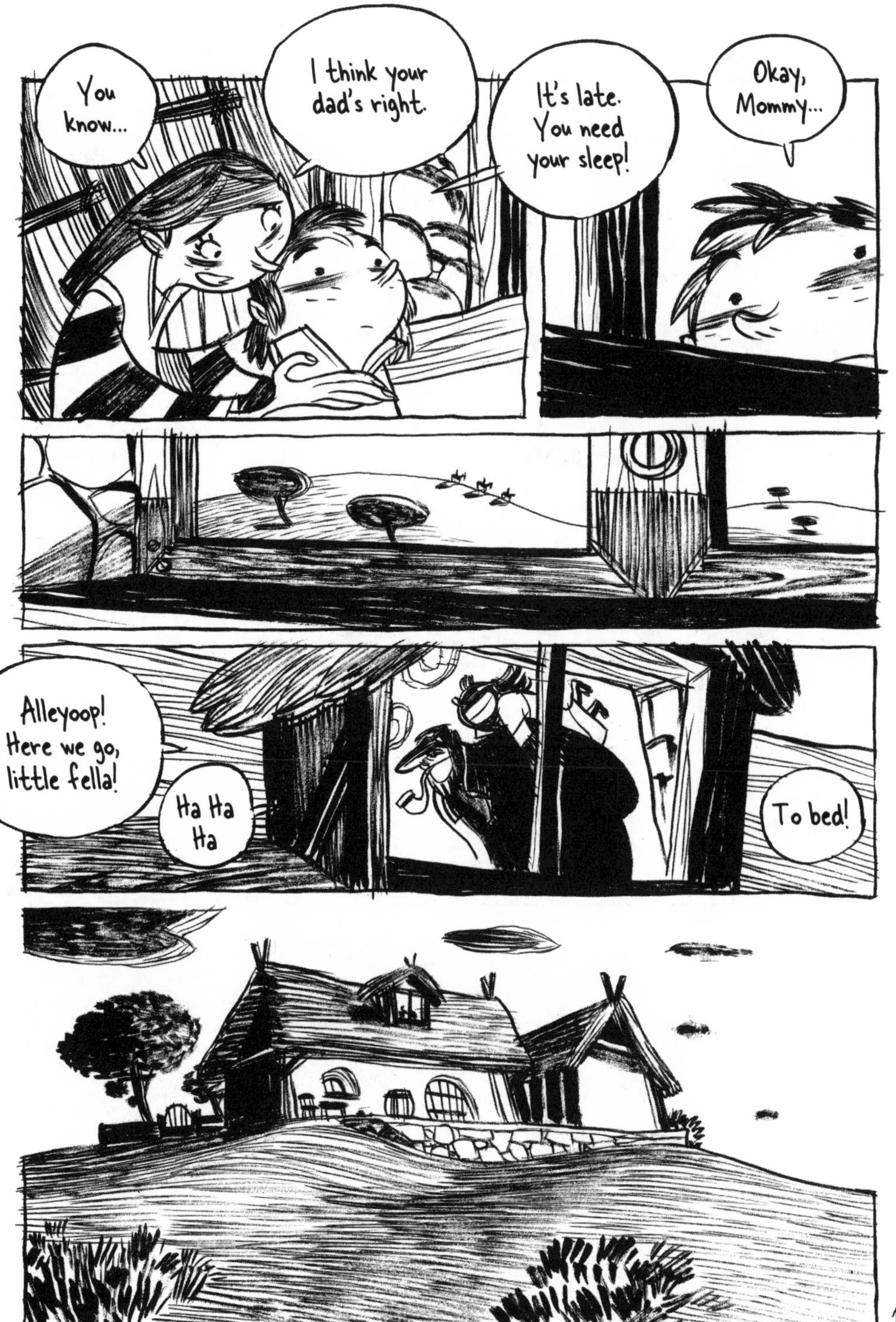
You know...
I think your dad's right.
It's late. You need your sleep!
Okay, Mommy...
Alleyoop! Here we go, little fella!
Ha Ha Ha
To bed!

Joachim!!
Hurry up, your father's waiting!
Comiiiing!

woof
woof

CHAAARRGE!
WOOF!

Yeehaa!
ha
ha
ha

hee hee hee
clippety
clop

Here, Mommy made you a sandwich.
Thanks!
Woof Woof
Crunch...
Woof Woof
Daddy?
Yes?
Ish iff far?
ha ha ha!
Don't talk with your mouth full.
No, it's not very far—don't you remember?
A little under an hour.

An hour?!
Does that mean we won't get there till after lunch?
No, before then.
I'm still hungry...
You just had a sandwich.
Yeah, but...
I think I want some sausage.
Tut tut
We'll stop and eat soon.

snap
rustle
snap
snap

Hmph.
Slim pickings!
Can I see?
Here.
Ewww!
Is it dead??
Can I touch it?
Of course you c—
WOOF WOOF WOOF
WOOF

WOOF
WOOF
WOOF
WOOF WOOF
WOOF
C'mon!
Let's see what's going on!
woof
woof
woof
CAW
WOOF
CAW
WOOF
WOOF

CAW
CAW
CAW
CAW
CAW
CAW
Grrr
Grrr
CAW
CAW
CAW

Good boy, Diego!
Let's take a look!
WOOF
WOOF
Good boy...
So...
What have we here?
Oh! Not our lucky day!...
What?
Look...
We caught a handsome jackrabbit...
But the crows got him first!

What?
Grrrrrr
What is it, boy?
Diego!!
WOOF WOOF
WOOF
WOOF
WOOF
WOOF
WOOF

DIIIIEEEEGOOO!
Diego...
We've gott go after him!
Hm...
The fog's set in quickly.
Can't see a thing now.
Oh well.
We'd better head back.
Poor Diego.
What's gonna happen to him?

Don't worry.
He knows the way better than I do.
He'll get home on his own.
You okay?
Not cold, are you?
Yeah.
A little...

Chomp
Chomp
Chomp
Mommy...
Do you thin
he'll find hi
way back?
I'm sure
of it!
Chomp
Chomp
Chomp
Say,
Bessie...
Not much
milk today!
Okay!
Chomp
Chomp
Chomp
Done!
That's it
for today!
whap

Have you ever gotten lost in the fog?
Yes, once, when I was little.
But—
I didn't have a nose like Diego's!
How big were you?
This big?
A little bigger!
Like this.
How did you find your way home?
Oh! Well, that's a long story.
In fact, I'd—

SPLASH
kling
klang
klang

They gave me such a fright!
Brrr...
Just thinking about them...
I don't get it...
They just sit there, unmoving...
What is it they want?
That does it!
I'm settling this, once and for all!

Wait, Louis!
It could be dangerous!
FOR CHRIST'S SAKE!!
I'M NOT GOING TO SIT IN MY HOUSE LIKE A FOOL JUST BECAUSE—
Can I go out too?
No, you're staying here.
It's too foggy out there.

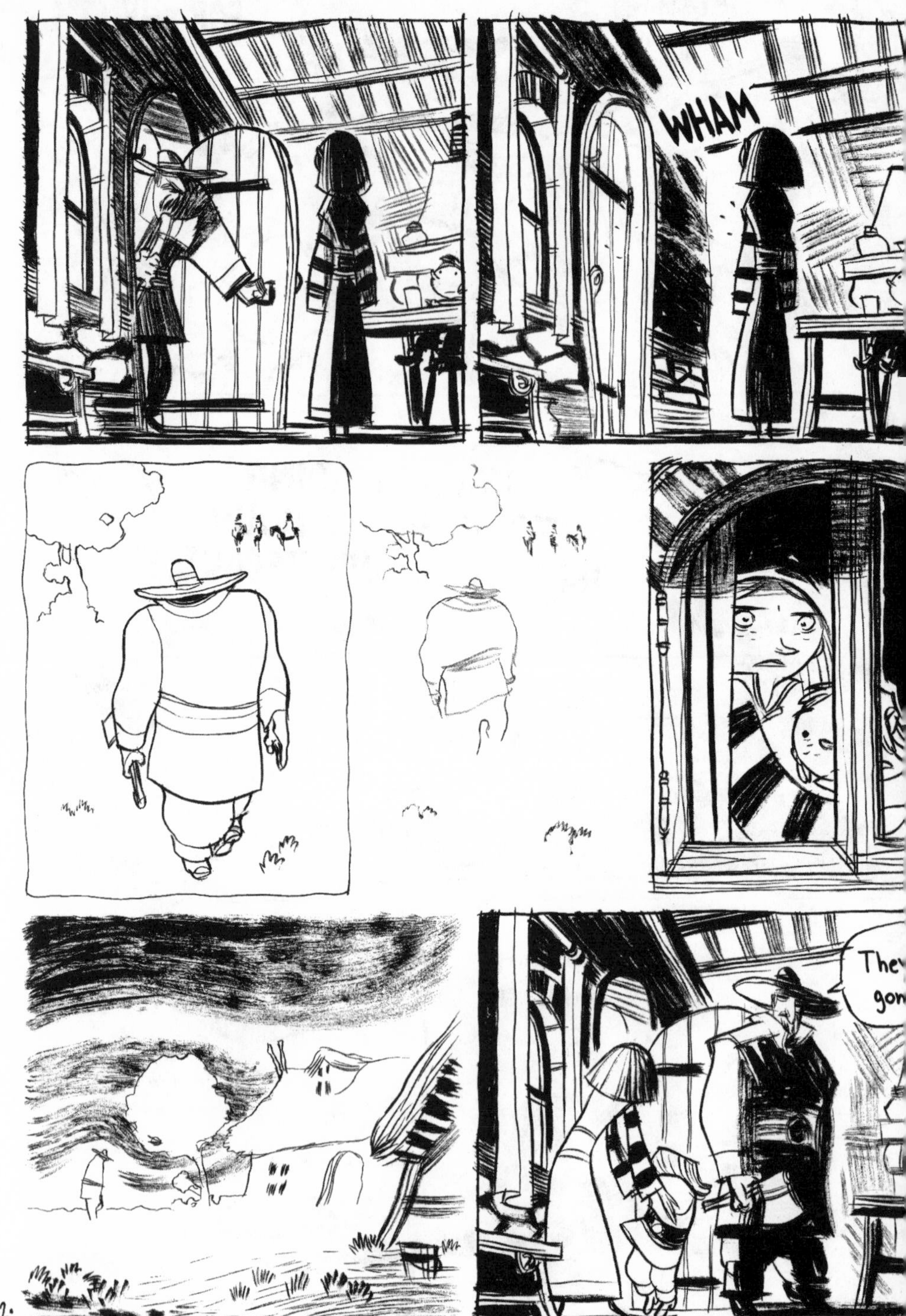
WHAM
The
go

I went toward them...
I called out...
Hmph.
Nothing.
Gone.
The fog's lifting.
Can I go out now?
Joachim...
Listen to me.
It's important...
From now on, I don't want you going out alone.
Ever!
Understand?
Yes, Father.

Louis...
...We can't go on like this!

Something must be done...

What would you have me do??
I don't know wha
they want.
They're like...
...eels.
The minute you tighten your grip—
—they
away!

Honestly...
...I just don't get it!
I was thinking...
I was thinking...that perhaps we might go see...
...Mistress Pike.
37.

THAT OLD PIKE HAG?
No way! Ab-so-lute-ly NOT!
Do you hear?
We don't need that crazy old woman's help to get rid of...
...of...
Yes, Louis?
To get rid...
...of what?
Of those...
...things...

CREAK

creak
creak
creak
creak
scrrrrrrr

glug
glug
glug
SCRITCH!
glug
glug
glug
Scritch
Scritch
Scritch
hooo hooo hooo hoooo
Diego?
Scritch
Scritch
Scritch

That you?
Scritch
Scritch
Scritch
Woof!
Diego!
Ha ha!
I'm coming, boy!
I'll let you in!
Scritch
Scritch
Scritch

Click!
C'm'ere, bo—
oof
oof

WHAM!

Sshhhh...
It's over.
I'm here.
There now...

huff
huff
...it's going to be okay...
Sshhh...
There there...
huff
huff
huff
huff
huff
GO AWAY!

GET OUT OF HERE, YOU—

KLING

kling
kling
klang
klang

Zzzzzz

woof
woof
woof
woof Woof
WOOF WOOF
Mom
Daddiee
Dad
Dad Mom
Mommm
49.

Mm mm...
Sshh...
Lise?

clip clop
clip clop

Crrrrrr

HEEE HAAAW!

Easy, Mabel...
Easy...
clip clop
clip clop

Louis,

Fear and anger won't protect Joachim.

We need to know.

I'll be back tomorrow.

I love you.

Lise

clip clop
clip clop

clip clop

clip clop

zzzzz...
zzzzz...
Alms!
mm...
gling gling
Shhh!
People trying sleep he
Haaave piteee on a poor blind man!
Shuuut up!!
clip clop clip clop clip

And you?

You can talk to flies?

Yes, I can!

I mean...

...almost...

Let's say I understand fly...

Actually...
Flies aren't very nice to me.
zzz

Psst!
Hey! Miss!
a want one?
Mmgnm...
Huh??
Wha—?
Dimitri!
Leave the lady alone!

Kof kof!

That boy wears me out!

teclop teclop

I didn't do nothin'!

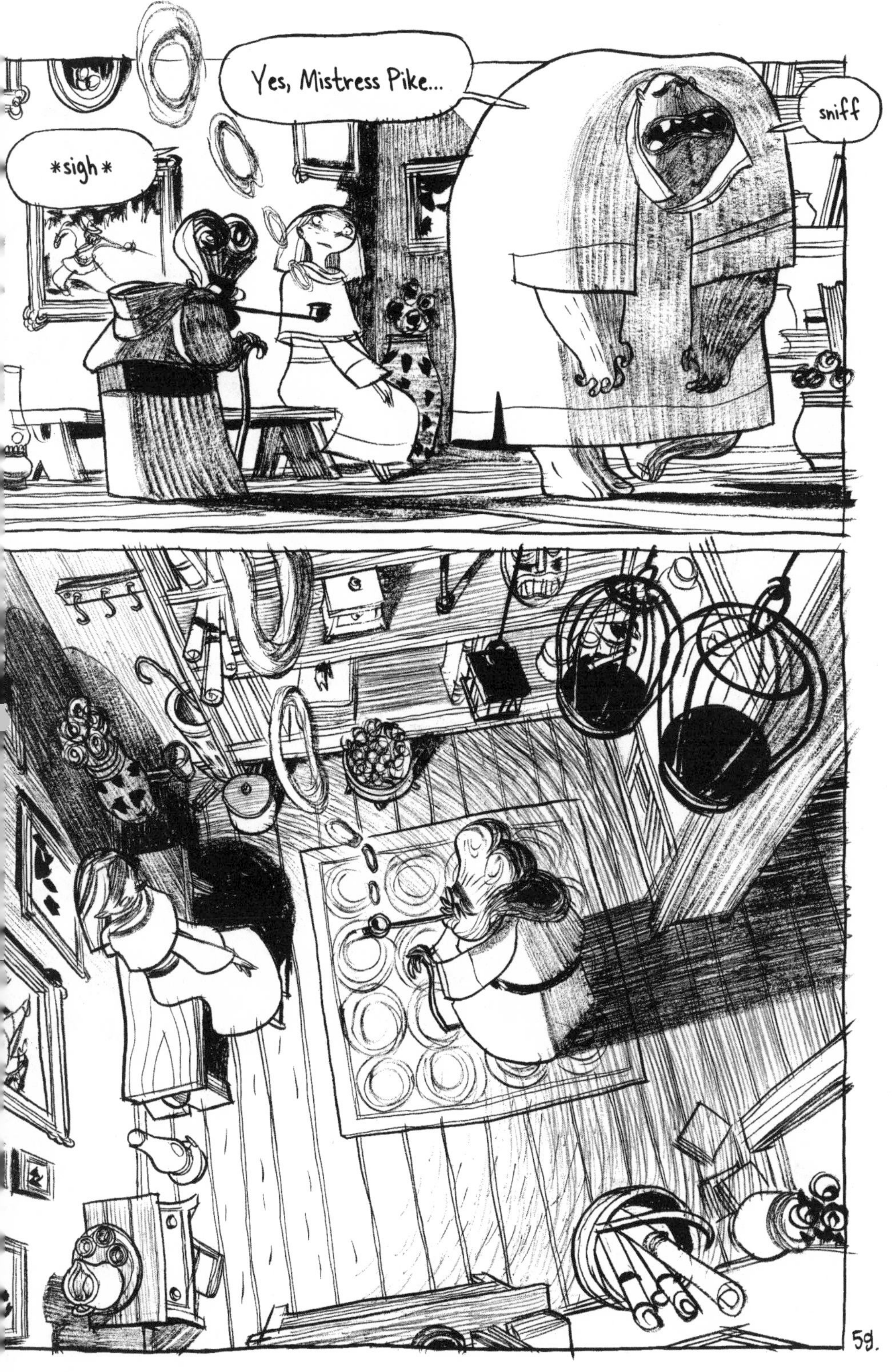
sigh
Yes, Mistress Pike...
sniff

Lise...
...my chickadee...
It's been so long.
I know...
So you've got a new tenant?
Dimitri?
Yes! He's a nice boy.
Give me a hand, would you?
Of course!
Are you okay?
Ohhhh. Yes, thanks.
This dratte old body's started playi tricks on me
So...
...what brings you to my house in the middle of the night?

My chickadee...

There, there... Tell me all about it.

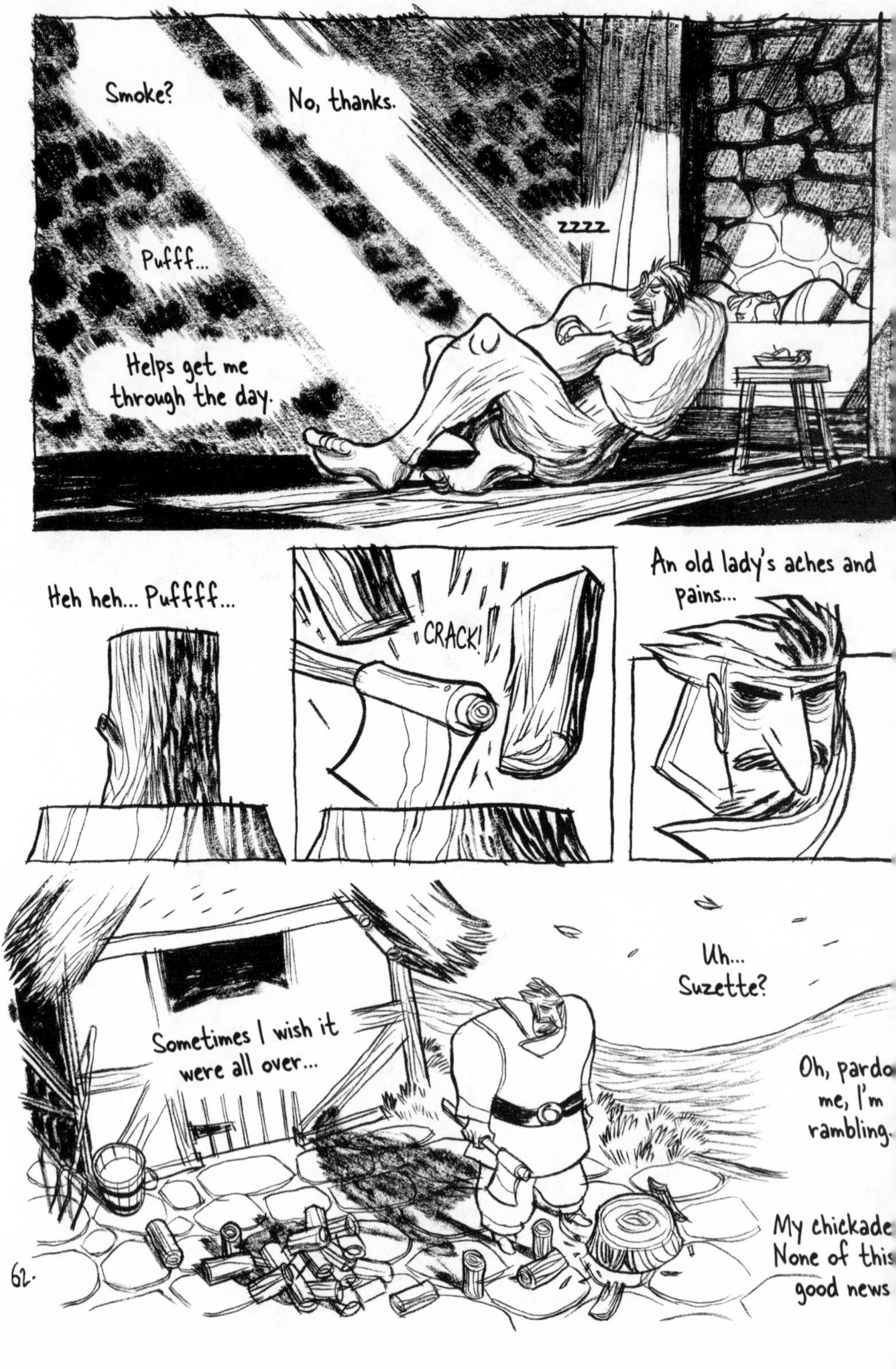

Smoke?

No, thanks.

ZZZZ

Pufff...

Helps get me through the day.

Heh heh... Puffff...

CRACK!

An old lady's aches and pains...

Uh... Suzette?

Sometimes I wish it were all over...

Oh, pardo
me, I'm
rambling.

My chickade
None of this
good news

Now, I may be mistaken...
...and I'm not even sure that—
Please...
I came to find out...
Hmf. Well. As you wish.
I believe these "things" have come for Joachim.
CRACK
Joachim? My God, what can—
Nothing. We can do nothing.

I–I don't understand...Joachim?! But why?
Take this journal. I've underlined a passage that will provide some answers.
But listen well, my chickadee: don't try to fight these "shadows"...it's no use.
Make the most of each moment...
...with Joachim...
Clip clop
...so long as he's with you...
I have to go.
Yes, of course.
Go back to them.

Did that crazy old bat put that in your head?

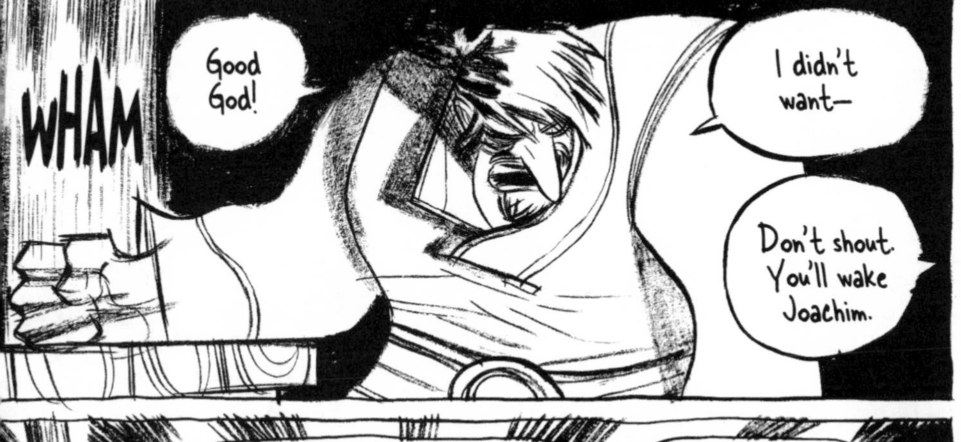
WHAM
Good God!
I didn't want—
Don't shout. You'll wake Joachim.

I...
I didn't want you to go see that old woman!
You didn't want me to...
...because you know she's right.
And you're angry...
...precisely because there's nothing you can do.

Louis...
Please...
No.
I won't let those "things" take my son.
Dad
Mommy...
Why are you fighting?
My darling...
Come here!

Puff
Puff
Puff

sigh

Puff
Puff

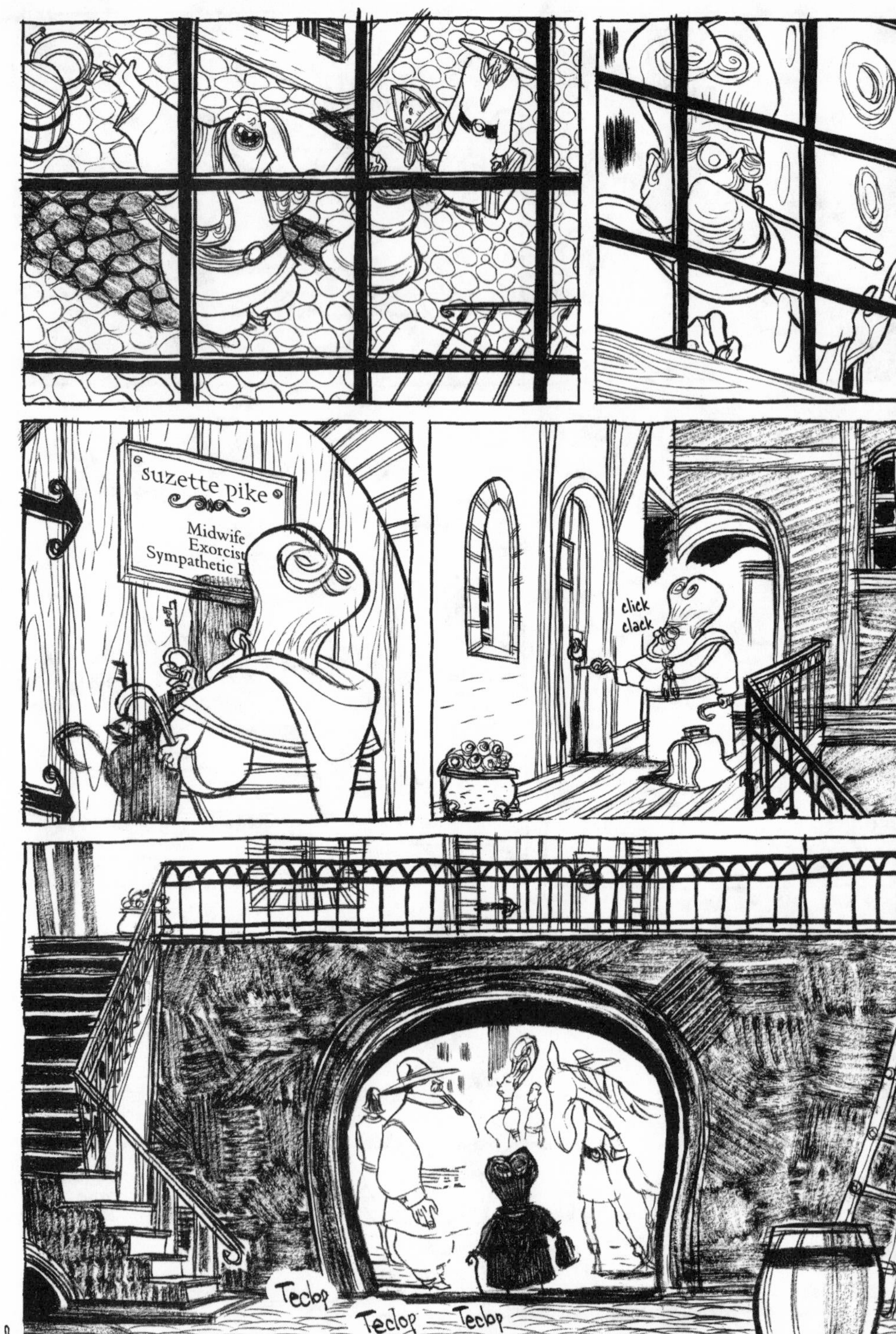
suzette pike
Midwife
Exorcist
Sympathetic
click
clack
Teclop
Teclop
Teclop

Teclop
Teclop
Teclop
Teclop
Teclop
splash
splash
Teclop
Teclop

They're really close tonight...
Louis...
Are you sure you want to leave now?

It's going to be foggy out there...
That'll help us.

I won't stop you from going, but I don't know if I'll be able to forgive you for it.

Joachim will leave us: I know this, and I'm prepared. Unlike you.

Lise...
Let me finish!

It probably won't be long before the shadows take him away.

These final moments with my son— this time...

I give to you.

So that when he leaves you, your heart...

...will be at peace.

I shall lose a son.

I hope we won't lose each other too.

huff
huff
huff

huff
huff
huff

huff
huff

hhhh...
hhhh...
hhhh...
hhhh...
hhhh...

huff
huff

suzette pike
Journal
XXIV.
Tuesday, September 2
Tuesday, September 2
Slept poorly. Dreamt of
the three shadows again...
A dream with such truth,
such memories, and such
precise details that it
terrified me...

Slept poorly...
Dreamt of the three shadows...
...again...
A dream filled with such truth...
...such memories...
...and such precise details...
...that it terrified me.

I spilled a bowl of boiling water.
I screamed.
I cried.
...My arm was covered in blisters.
This pain...
...that won't stop.

Mother slept beside me...
She saw nothing.
Yet the shadows were there...
...waiting...
...sitting by the bedside
like three vultures on a branch.
I wanted to cry out...
...but I couldn't.

I have awaited you...
...for so long...

This time...
I'm ready...
hhh
hhh
hhh
hhh

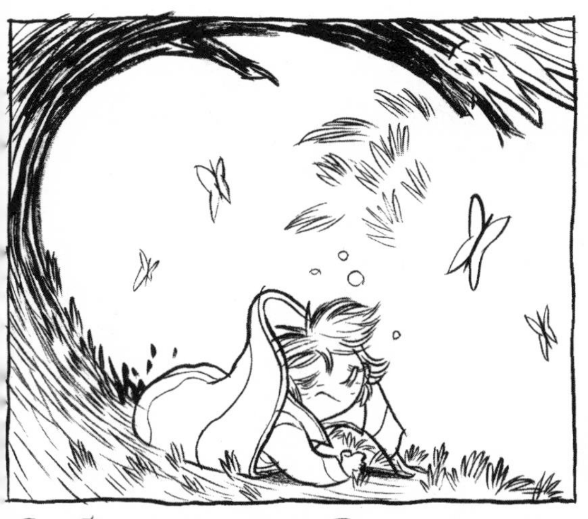

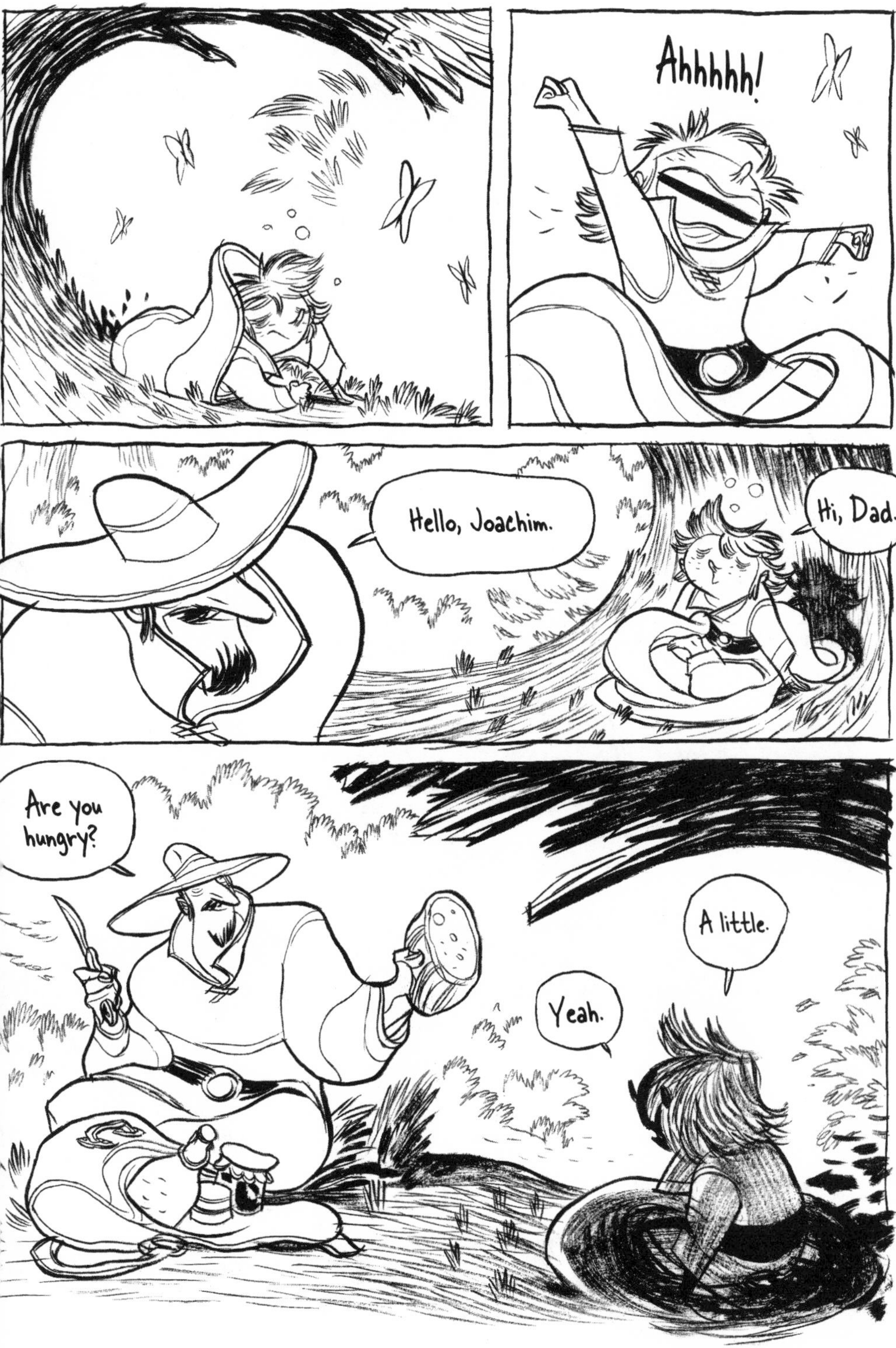

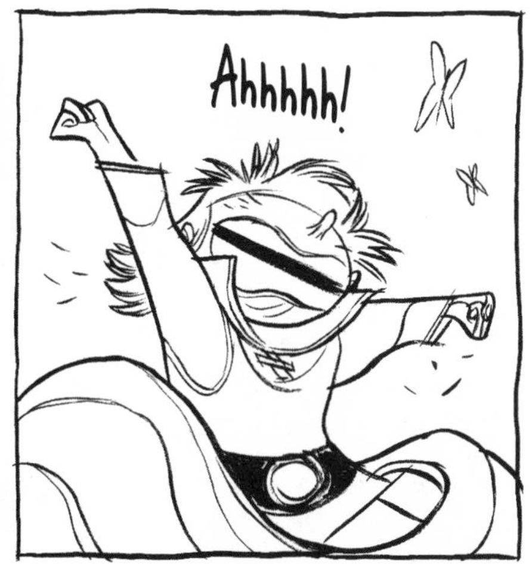
Ahhhhh!

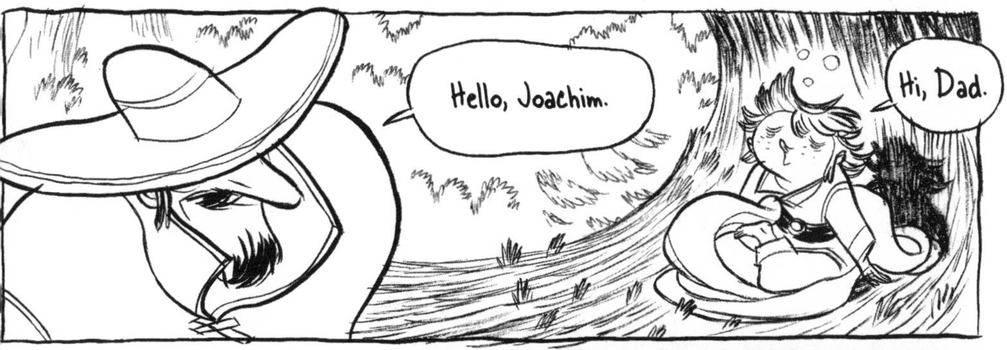
Hello, Joachim.
Hi, Dad.

Are you hungry?

A little.

Yeah.

Crunch
Crunch
Crunch
Crunch
Crunch
Daddy?
Yes?
What're we doing here?

I know I could have lied...

...but I didn't.

Joachim listened closely.

I have no doubt he perfectly understood the stakes of our journey.

Still, we hit the road again with light hearts.

Our fear had left us.

After walking for a day, I knew why.
Perhaps it wouldn't last, but for now the shadows had stopped trailing us.

Tomorrow we'll head west, toward the river.
Then what?
Then we'll cross the river, and keep heading west.
That's where your randfather's from.
We'll be safe there.
Oh good...
What's it like across the river?
I don't know.
I've never been.

Well?
I've never seen a river so wide!
hehe...
Pretty, isn't it?
Yeah.
How'll we cross it?
We'll take the ferry.
There's a landing a bit further down the bank.

n your grandfather's time, it took three days to cross.
It's probably the same today.
If we grab a boat before the shadows catch up, we'll have a six-day lead.
And be out of their reach!
Daddy—
I'm a little tired.
I know. We'll sleep on the boat, kiddo.
Ready?
Holding on tight?
Yeah!
Let's go!
YAHOOOO
ha ha ha

Fresh water! Fresh water!!
WAAAH
What do you mean, you "forgot" your bag?
Just wait'll I get my hands on you, you—

dy?
Is it much farther?
Hmm...
I don't know...
All these people!
It's making me dizzy.
Do you see something?
Yeah!!
Way over there!
A bunch of people in a long line...
Well that must be the—
Out of the way, fatso!
Aaaah!

Idiot!
Joachim!!
OW!
You all right?
ow ow ow
Yeah, I'm okay...
But my butt hurt
Heh
Ha Ha Ha
Hee Hee
Well!
Let's go check out the line.
Heh
Mommmmieee—

Mommmmieee—
Mommy, where are yooou?
Hmm.
Let's tie ourselves together, okay?
That way, we'll be sure not to lose each other.
Okay, Dad.

Keep an eye on your bag!
I hafta go pee...
Well, you'll have to wait.
moo
But I really hafta—
Moo
Stop pushing!
I can't take this, Victor, let's go home
You're not going to start that again.
MOOO
Oh yes I am.
They told me it'd be a hard crossing, but really...
...for two days...
sigh
I didn't expect crowd like this.

On the
her hand...
it makes us
rder to find.
But I wonder if...
Excuse me?
You in the trade too?
I stopped handling kids.
Too fragile.
Too many losses.
Now I just work with the ladies!
ve got a good client
wn south who orders
some every month!
Between you and me, he goes through a lot...
I'd rather not know what he does with them!

But—
You're not going to sell her like cattle?
Uh—
How else am I going to sell her?
Number 175!!
Aha!
That's me!
Lessee...What did I do with that—?
Here we are!
175
See ya later!
On th
boat
175
RE
'Scuse me.
Number 175 here.
'Scuse me.
Daddy?
Do we have a ticket too?

No.
Dear God.
If I'd known about all this...
Tickets are up at the front of the camp.
In the shed.
Thanks, ma'am.
Come, Joachim.
Let's go.
Thanks.
You're welcome.
Good luck.

KNOCK
KNOCK
KNOCK

Hmm...
WOOF
WOOF
WOOF

WHAM
WHAM
WHAM

...es? What is it?
WOOF
WOOF
WOOF

Oooh!
SHUT IT, NEPTUNE!
SIT!

Yes?
Uh...
Do you have any... tickets?
Ah! One moment, please.

SLAM!!
Grrrrr

woof
woof
woof

Sorry to have kept you waiting.
Come in, sir.
Come in
Let me just show these ladies out, and I'll be right with you.
COMPANY
Tip Tap Tip Tap Tip Tap Tip Tap

Wait here, my sweet.
WHAM!
So...
You're here for...tickets?
Is that it?
Exactly.
Ha ha, of course!
No ticket, no boarding pass!
meow
And no boarding pass...
meow
...no crossing!
Ha ha!
Yes...
We all know how it works.

You're in luck!
I've still got two tickets left...
...for next month's ferry.
But—
—we can't—
You don't understand!!
We can't wait until next month! We—it's—
Ohh...I see.
So it's a matter of life and death.
Isn't it?

Hmm...
Perhaps there's a way...
There's always a way.
How much?
All of it.

clack
I don't know what's keeping me from—
Ah-ah-ah
I kno
flap flap
Isn't that right, my boy?

Go on—
Now beat it.
198.
197.
197
198

PONK
Okay.
Go on in.
Thank you.
whew!
This time we've—
...
Joachim—
It's over now.
I wanted to...sniff...
I wanted to kill him!

Don't say such things.
The shadows haven't followed us.
That's the most important thing.

Zzzzzzzz...
Sshhh...
Kof...
Koff...
Zzzzzzzz...
Mommy?
What's the matter?

Zzzzzzz...

I wanna throw up.

Zzzzzzzz...

Drink some water.

It'll make you feel better.

Is that better?
glug glug glug
Mommy...
I don't feel good either.
Zzzz
Will someone shut those kids up?
You're one to talk!
What's with the wench?
Got a problem?
I sure do!
Mister Snore-All-Night telling other people to be quiet, really—!
Hic Hic
Huh!
And I was so sur
she was here.

Oh, you too?
I had this feeling someone was prowling around last night.
Did you see anything?
Aaachoo!
Bless you.
Not a thing. But—
It's high time we hit shore. We're not in very good company here.
Charms?
Amulets?
Evil eye...Storms... Broken hearts...
Ask for my magic amulets.
You got anything for seasickness?

Look—I've got pretty silver rings to settle the stomach.
I'll give you a good price.
This boat's hardly moving.
Yeah...
Two days without wind...i just takes so lon
I didn't think you could get sick in such calm waters.
Dad?
I'm still hungry.
Joachim, I just made you a sandwich.
Yeah, but I'm still hungry.

My little trooper...
You know...
We need to be careful with our food.
t seems the crossing
ill be longer than
expected.
And I don't want you—
hee hee
Go ahead, carinho, try some.
They're blackberries.

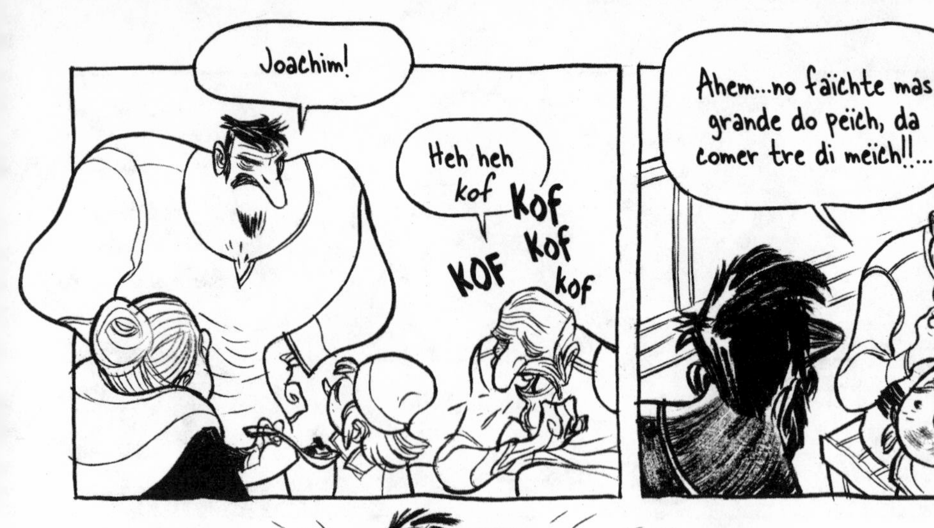

Joachim!
Heh heh kof
KOF
Kof Kof kof

Ahem...no faïchte mas grande do peïch, da comer tre di meïch!!...
kof

ha ha ha ha!

Are you from around here?
My father was.
I was born on the other side of the river.
Kof Kof kof

So...you've come ba
to the old countr
heehee...

Yes...you could say that.

We're headed back home.
It's been so long.
Can you imagine?
Yes—I think so.
Would you like to join us?
We've got some churasco left!
All right...
My thanks.
Here...
I've got some bread.

Dad?
Whaf did thaf man shay to you earlier? I couldn't understand.
Heh heh—
That you were as small as a bleakfish—
—but ate enough
three sea bass!
Welf I don' shee whafs so funny about that...
It's a saying they have around here.
Your grandfather used to say it too.

KOF KOF KOF KOF
Kof Kof
It'll pass.
KOF KOFF Kof
Easy there.
...as he been
...e this long?
Kof Kof Kof
querinha...
Ever since we got on the boat.
We're too old to sleep out in the open.
When I have a cough—
Mom makes me a poultice.
Kof Kof Kof
But how would we heat cloth for bandages?
The boy's right: poultices are useful.

Hmm...
We should be able to find a way.
I'll ask around.
Can you watch over Joachim for me?
Oh yes! Gladly.
Tell me, Joachim, do you also like strawberry jam?
Well...I'm not that hungry anymore.
But I'll try some.
heh heh...
Stay here. I'll be right back.

Sister, don't fall for a sailor...

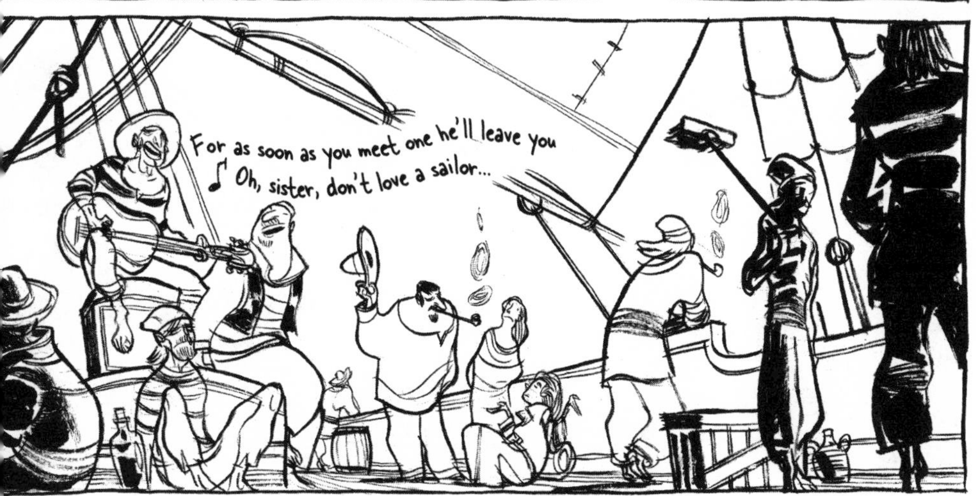

For as soon as you meet one he'll leave you
Oh, sister, don't love a sailor...

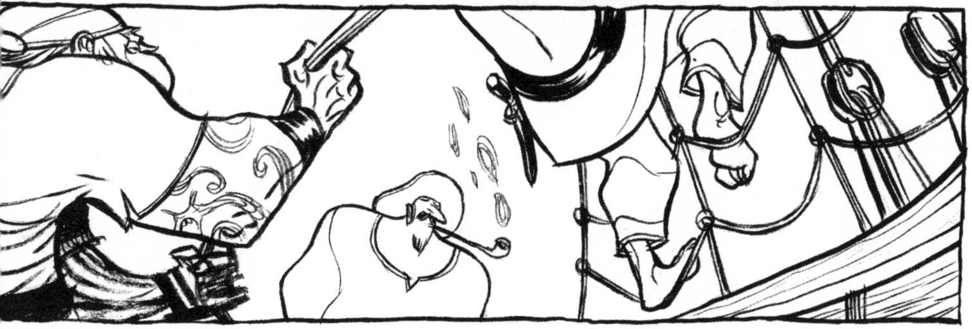

Poultices??
Gee...
I dunno...
Better ask the bosun.
Yeah!
Which one's he?
That big guy with the mustache over there.
Which one?
The one in t
jacket?

Yeah, that one. Ha ha ha...
...The one who's all dolled up.
HA HA HA HA
ha ha ha ha ha ha
Poultices?
Hmm... yes...
Might have to take that up with the captain.

It's for a sick old man.
We just need to warm up some bandages!
Right, I get it.
But all special requests go through the captain.
I'll take you to his cabin.
Oh don't make that face at me.
Hope the wind picks up. It's making everyone sick.
I'm not complaining.
At least no one's died yet

People die on the boat??
All the time.
It's like they come on board just to kick the bucket.
Pests.
These are poor
eople here. Most
them are hungry,
frightened, or...
Yeah.
That's what I said.
They come on board just to croak.
It's no fun throwing them overboard, I tell you.
No.
I don't imagine it is...

You're like me.
A sensitive soul.
Say...
If I may...
What?
What do you think of my jacket?
Your jacket?
Frankly.
I don
know
...hand
some?
Hmm...that'd be the embroidery.
It bother you too?

I hesitated a bit.
I wasn't sure...
t's silk hread.
Perhaps it's too dainty for a man's jacket?
Well.
I'll leave you now.
Uh...
I would've liked to see the captain...
He's just behind that door.
Ah.
All right.
Thanks...
Knock
Knock
Knock
Come in!

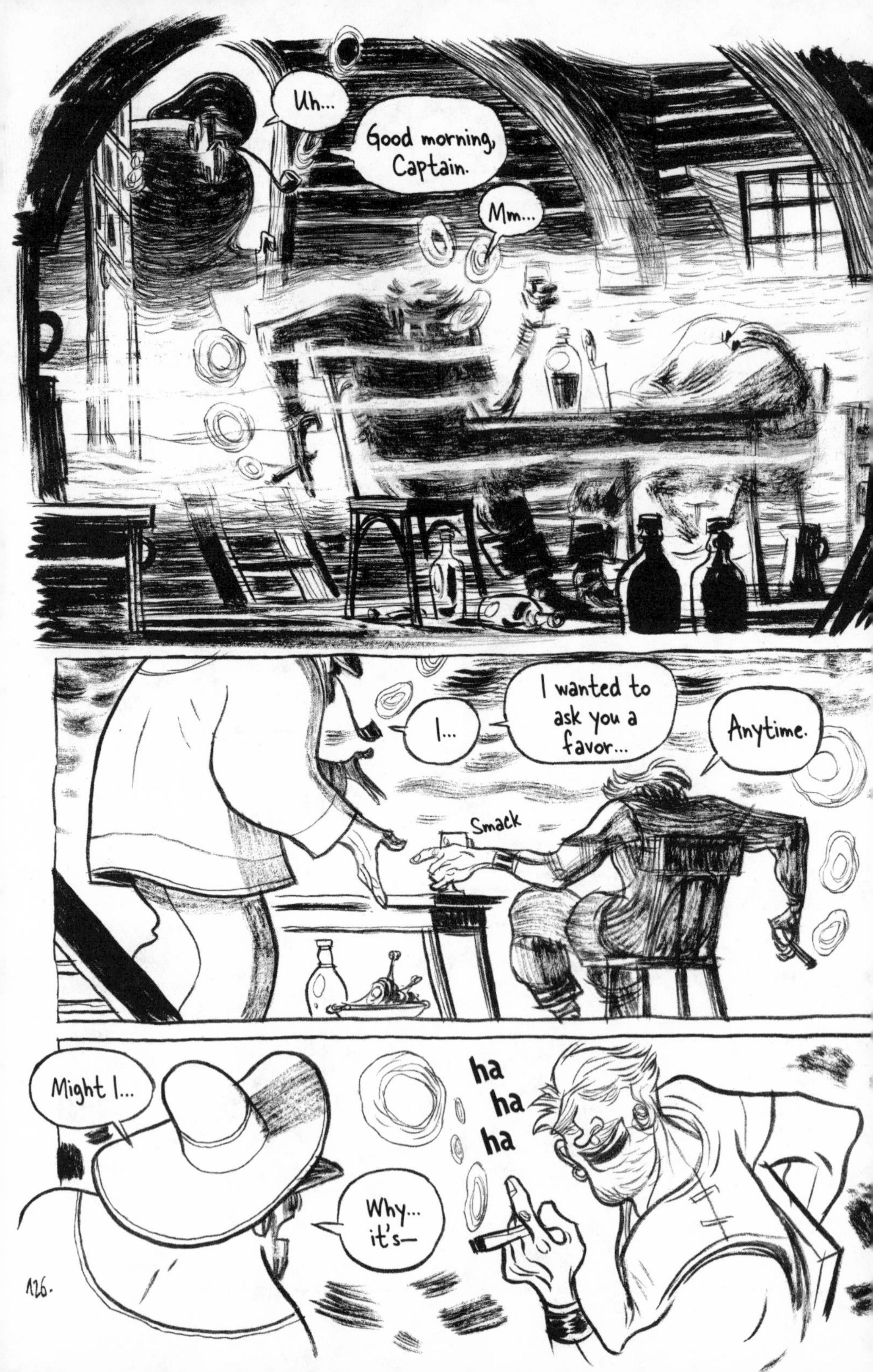
Uh...
Good morning, Captain.
Mm...
I...
I wanted to ask you a favor...
Anytime.
Smack
Might I...
ha
ha
ha
Why... it's—

Had ya, didn't I?
ha ha
ha ha
Zzzzzz
…just that…
…you wanted to see the captain?
Um…well, I mean…
Yes.
Well, my friend, looks like you're gonna have to come back later.
Here!
The only captain on board's sleeping like a baby!
Zzzz
Zzzz
ha ha
ha ha

glug glug
GlugGlugGlug
dah
What a night!
Between you and me, this young man held his own!
Zzzz
Zzzz
Zzzz
A good gambler!
A very good gambler!
Zzzz
Ding kling

But not much of a drinker!
ha ha ha
Zzzz
clink
I'll come back later...
Wait! I'm coming too.
Bit of fresh air would do me good.
Wait right there...
I'll get my jacket.
Zzzz zzzzzzz
Ding kling

Ding
kling
Ding
kling

Found it!

All set!
Couldn't find my treasure.
Heh...
Come!
ha ha ha
Tell me all about just why it was you wanted the captain!
WHAM!

Mmmm....
Still no wind, eh?
Does she stay chained up...all the time?
Who?
Oh—the girl?
I let the captain rent her for the crossing.
In exchan
for a goo
cabin.
Don't look at me like that.
She cooks and cleans, that's all.
If he touches her—
I'll kill him.

You have strange moral values.
I've got a businessman's values.
My client only buys virgins.
You're the one who should be killed...
Perhaps.
But that wouldn't change anything for her...
And besides...
I'm not sure murder's more moral than the slave trade.

Ahhh, "morals."
Frankly, just getting by in this world, such as it is, is enough trouble.
I haven't run into you since we left. Were you avoiding me?
We were sleeping on deck.
You're not really in the trade, are you?
Listen—
I don't know what you're up to with your little kid.
But if you care about him, don't stay on deck.

The captain predicts bad weather for tonight or tomorrow.
It's going to be hell belowdecks.
Amulet?
Guaranteed protection!
I don't have a choice.
At any rate, I—
Looking for adventure?
I'm sure you'd like to know—
No thanks.

You need help. All men have problems.
Leave me be!
And yours are far from over...
Stop it!
Ggg-gguuh-guh-gaah ggggg...
Something follows you... you think you can escape it, but—
ENOUGH!!

LEAVE US BE, BITCH!

You are making waaay...
...too much noise.
Manfred—
Please put your knife away.
Let her finish the crossing in the hold, so I never have t see her on the bridge again.
We'll get rid of this riffraff.

DIE, dirty dog!
Shut it.
But...
You didn't have to go and do that!
She lived off other people's fears.
I find that despicable.
Of course.
You, who live off other people's suffering.
That's much nobler.

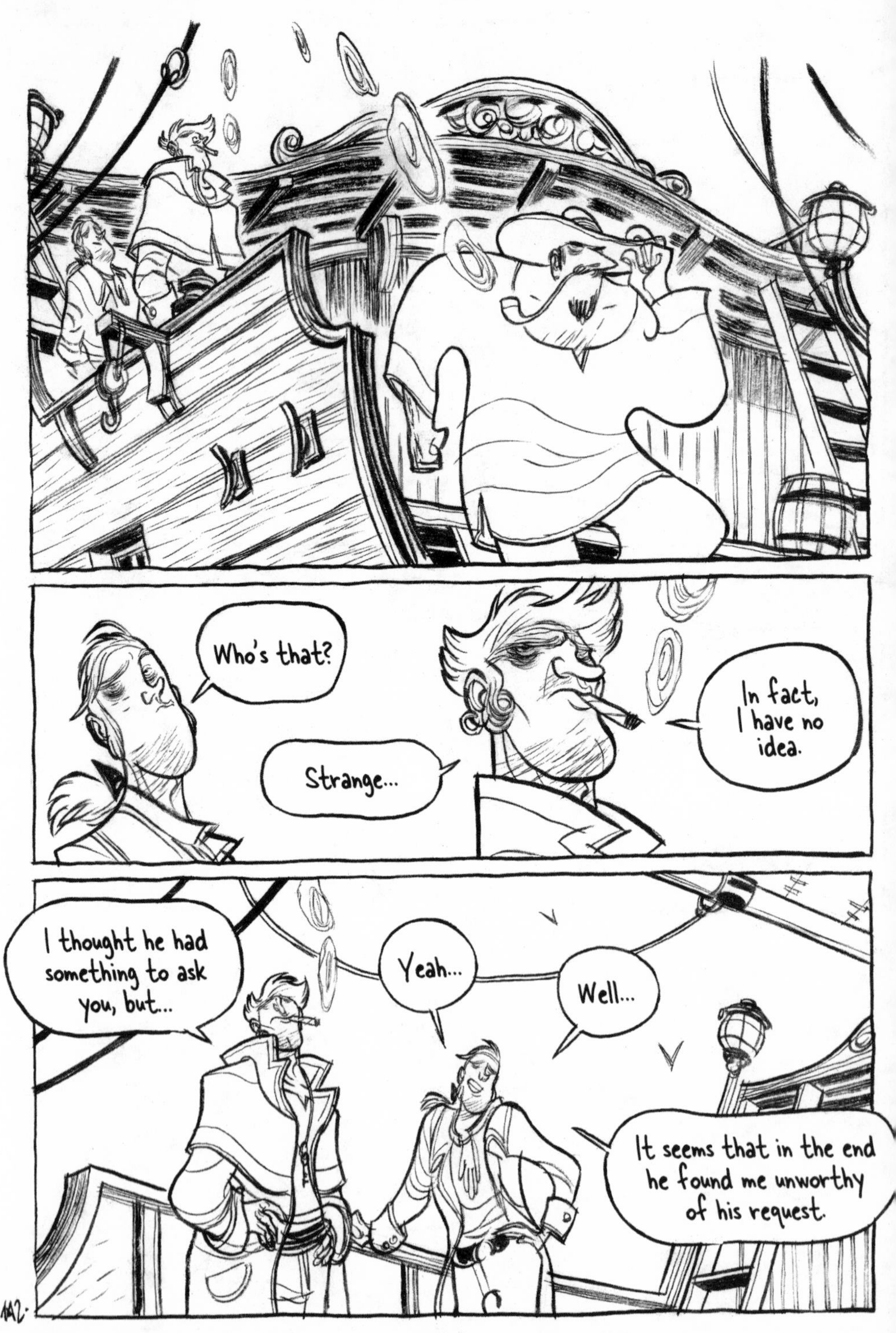

Who's that?
Strange...
In fact, I have no idea.
I thought he had something to ask you, but...
Yeah...
Well...
It seems that in the end he found me unworthy of his request.

Yep.
What a hoity-toity!
ha ha ha
I tell you this in friendship, Manfred...
I'd rather you didn't kill anyone on my boat.
You'd find the brig uncomfortable.
Don't worry.
I intend to enjoy my cabin to the fullest.
Anyway, I'm not done cheating you at cards...ha ha ha!
Are you joking?!
Truth is, you had a brazen run of luck last night!
That kind of luck doesn't come around twice...

kof
kof
kof

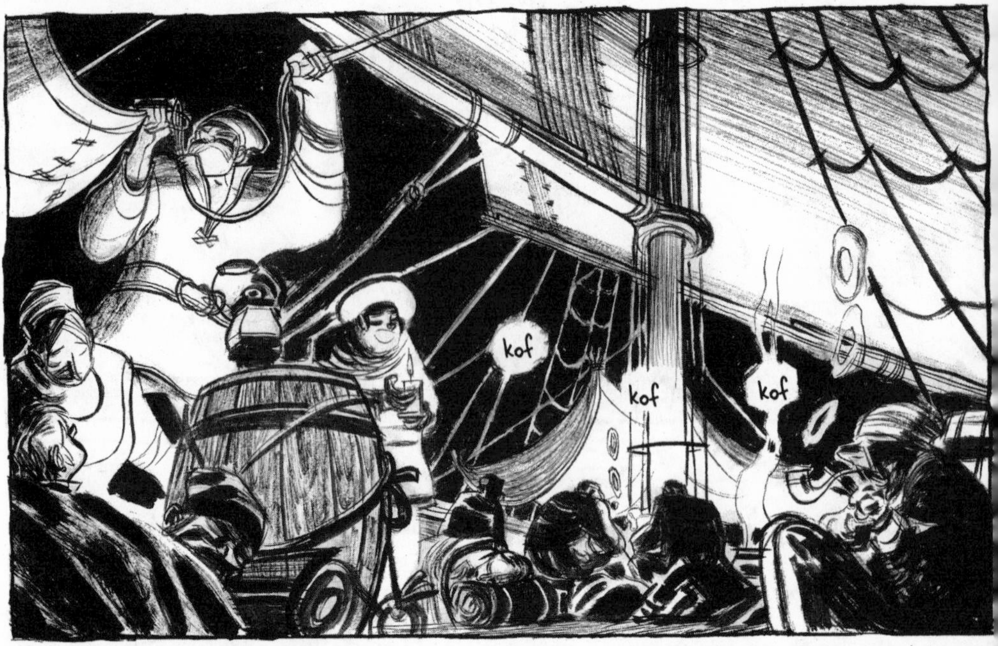

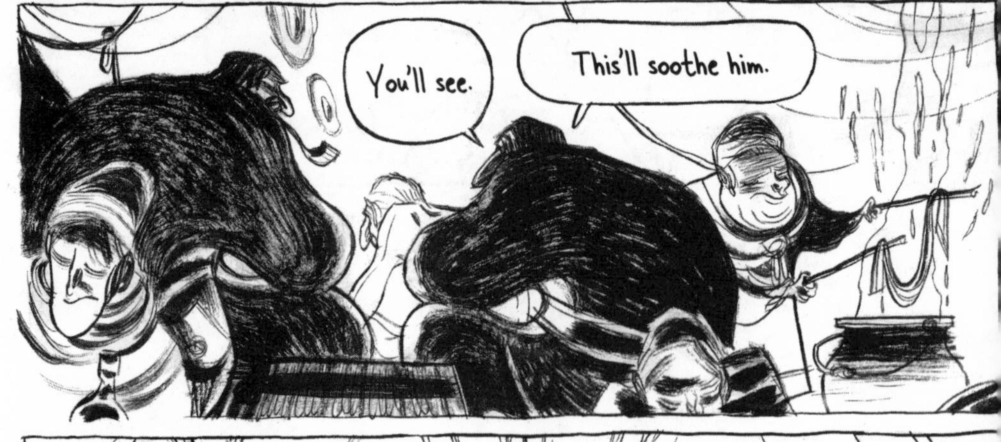
You'll see.
This'll soothe him.

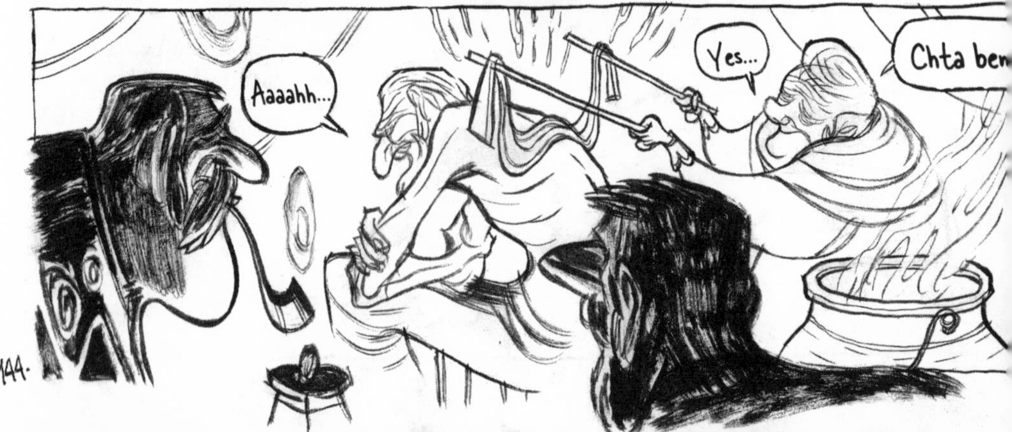
Aaaahh...
Yes...
Chta be

Well, I'll leave you to it.
I'm going to check on the boy.
kof kof
Uh—
Sure...it was nothing.
Aaahhh.
kof kof
Thanks again for the hot water.
Good night!
zzzzz
sshhh!!

You okay?
Not too cold?
I'm okay, Dad.
You're safe here.
Sleep well, now. I'll be right by you.
Dad?
Do you think Giuseppe'll get better?
I hope so, son.
We're taking care of him, you know.
Now go to sleep, it's late...
fff

Dad?
Do you think the shadows'll come back?

I'd like to go home and see Mom now.

Sshhh...
Everyone's sleeping.
We'll go back once we're sure it's safe, understand?
Yes, Dad.

kling
ding

HIC
ha ha ha
Bravo! Hats off, my little captain!

When your luck has turned, it's time to stop!

Back to my quarters now!
hic!
G'night, Manfred!

Good niiight sweet captaaain!

hee hee hic!

Good night, everyoone! ♪

hhhh

ha ha ha

ha ha ha

hhhh
BAM
hhhh
hhhh

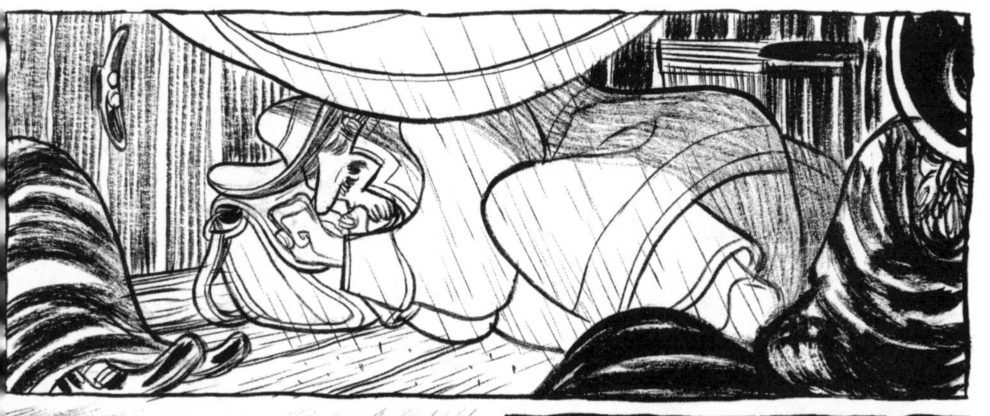

DIE, FOUL DOG!!
BOOM!
Hrm...?

Hrmm...
ZZZZ...
Hurry!
We can't stay here!
Coming...

I represent the law on this ship—
Even our nation's authority.
As such...
I must be unyielding.

Those behind this crime will be put in irons and handed over to the port authority...
Daddy! I can't see anything!
Good.
And swiftly hanged from a short rope!
Thanks to this young woman, who knew the victim—
We know that several valuable items were stolen from him.
It was a heinous crime.

I ask your cooperation in emptying your bags and pockets before the crew.
Let's get it over with.
I'd be surprised if we found anything...
...but a little show of force never hurt anyone.

This way, please...

Single file, or we'll never finish...

No, this way!

C'mon!
Keep it moving!
Above all, don't let go of my hand!
Yes, Dad.
And stick with me during the search!
Yeah, Dad.
You're fine.
This line's not moving at all!
Chta bem.

Zzz
Zzz
Zzz
WHAP!
Missed.
LET ME GO!!
LET GO, I SAID!
dy!
Don't you dare touch my son!
Did you find some-thing??
Well...
Uh...
This!

I have no idea what that is!
Someone must've slipped it in my pocket!
Of course.
Hm...
Well.
Do you recognize this object?

Yes.

Well.
Anything to add?
I didn't do it.
Mm.
I doubt that'll be enough to keep you from hanging.
Lock him up until we land.
What a pity.

I won't let you hang that child!
What is it now?
Who are you? His grandmother?
My little Joachinho...
Do you know this woman, kid?
Do you want to stay with her?
I want my daaaddiee!
sigh
At any rate, we'll hand them over to the authorities tomorrow. It won't be my problem anymore.
Until then, if he wants his last few moments with his father—
Well, I won't deprive him of that.

SAINTS ALIVE!
What the hell are you doing there??
I said:
Everyone in the rigging!!

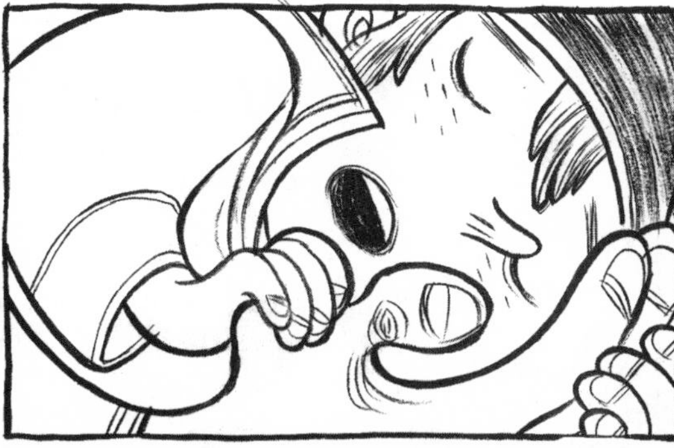

The shadows...
They were here.

I saw them last night...
They killed that man!

Dear God...

Have mercy on us.

VLAAAM!!

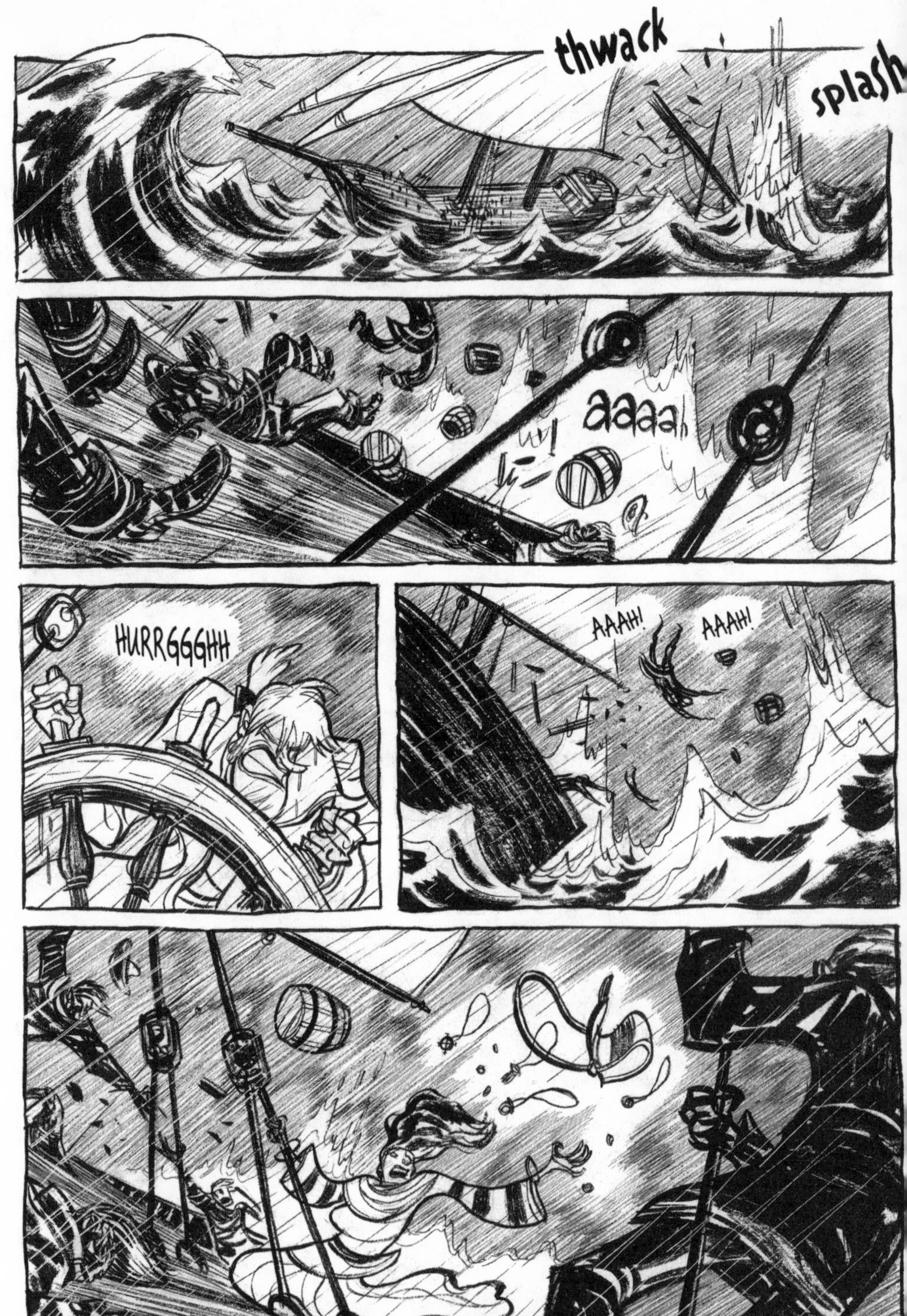
thwack
splash
aaaah
HURRGGGHH
AAAH!
AAAH!

TURN, YOU–

Ding!
Ding!
Ding!

Ding!
Ding!
Ding!
Ding!

Ding!
Ding!
Breach!
Breach!
To the rafts!
We're sinking!

Kling
Klong
Klang

Hurry!! Get out!
Daddy? What going on?

I'm warning you: if your captain thinks—
The captain's dead.
We must leave now!
Come!
You aren't a killer.
The captain—
They've killed him too!
They followed us all the way here! They brought death, and the storm!!
Do you understand?
Enough!
I don't know what you're talk-ing about, and I don't care!
You have to go!
The ship's sinking!

It's no good.
We can't escape them.
Where would you have us go?
INTO THE WATER, FOR CHRIST'S SAKE!
JUMP NOW!

Do you hear me?
JUMP!

Yes...
Yes, all right.

What-
about you?
I have to make sure everyone's gone first.

The water's not that cold.
Hang on to a plank—
And you'll reach land.
Did you hear, Joachim? We have to jump.
I'm scared.
It'll be okay.
It'll be just like when we jump into the pond, remember? Don't let go of my hand, all right?
sniff... Yes, Daddy...

Good luck!

kof kof
WOOF
WOOF

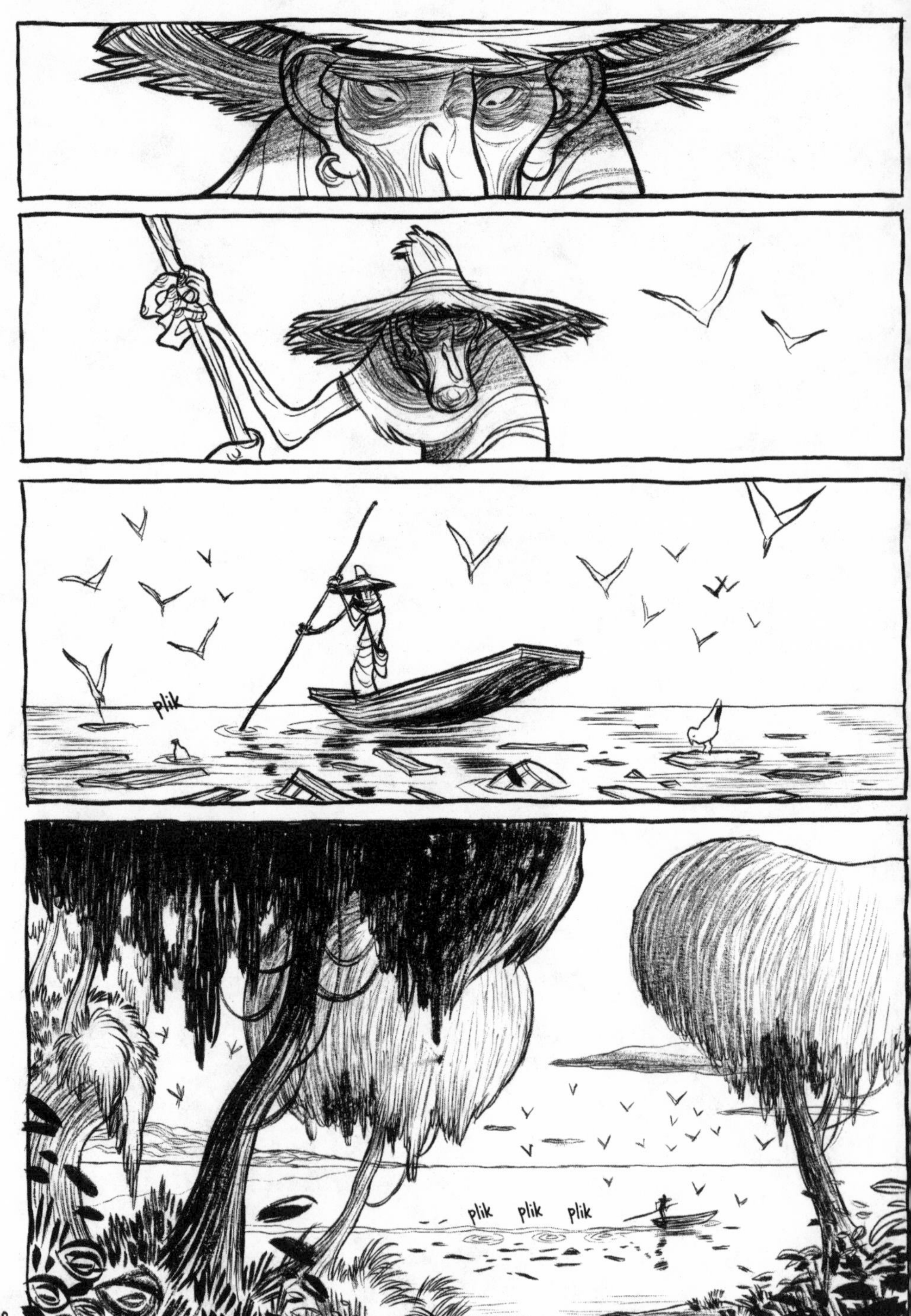
plik
plik plik plik

mmh...
rmm...

Ssshhh...
Hrggh
Relax...

You're safe here.
The little boy too.

Sshh...
Duerme chtino.

♪ Dueeeerme... do noïte na vench... ♪
♪ Dueeeerme... do noïte na vench mastina

drip
drip
drip

Careful.
It's hot.

You okay?
kof kof kof
Yes.

Thank you.

Go back to sleep.

plurk

kof
kof

How's the boy?
So?
Much better.
The fever's broken, but he's still tired.
Good.
I wanted to say...
For Joachim and myself... I know that without you...
Sluuurp
You owe me nothing.
I went back to the river this morning.
And—?

I found nothing.
That can't be—

KOF KOF KOF KOF
Tut tut—you shouldn't have sat up.
You still need sleep.

kof kof kof
There must've been a hundred passengers...
They couldn't all have—kof kof

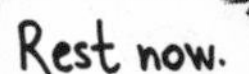

Rest now.
The river is vast...capricious.
Crisscrossed by complex forces and currents. And not everyone would have jumped at the same spot...
But there, where I found you, there was no one else.
Of that I am certain.

Drink.

It will make you feel better.

Kof Kof

It's all my fault.

Those... "things" followed us.
They killed the slave trader.
Then the captain...
...then all the passengers.
See here, the storm—
No.
They're shadows.
They're here.
They're stalking us.
me now...Look around you.
Where are the ghosts you speak of?
You yourself see there are none.
And anyway, who would come all the way here?

I'm an old man now.
I have nothing anymore. I am of interest to no one.
You don't understand.
They're after Joachim.
There's nothing to be done.
All that time wasted, running away. We fled in vain.
Look at this fire, this warmth...
...my sleeping son...
I now know just how precious such moments are...

It's time for us to go home.
To my wife, so together we might share what could still be...
Hmm...
...and the "shadows"?
don't now.
We'll see...
Not long ago, I would have given anything to save Joachim. But now...
You would have given...
...your life?
Without hesitation.
Well, then...
...perhaps there is something I can do for you.

What're you—
hhhh
Your heart is broken.
It's no longer worth much.
But I would buy it from you.
To help yo
At a good price, too.

For this beating heart I would give you the strength and power you need to save your little boy.

Daddy!

Don't do it!

unhh

unhh

Please.

It scares me.

Go back to sleep, Joachim.
But Daddy...

BACK TO SLEEP!!

You say that...I could save Joachim?
You would have the strength and power to do so—I promise.
No.
It can't be...
No one can do that.
Don't you even want to try?
Very well.
Go ahead.
— I'm ready.

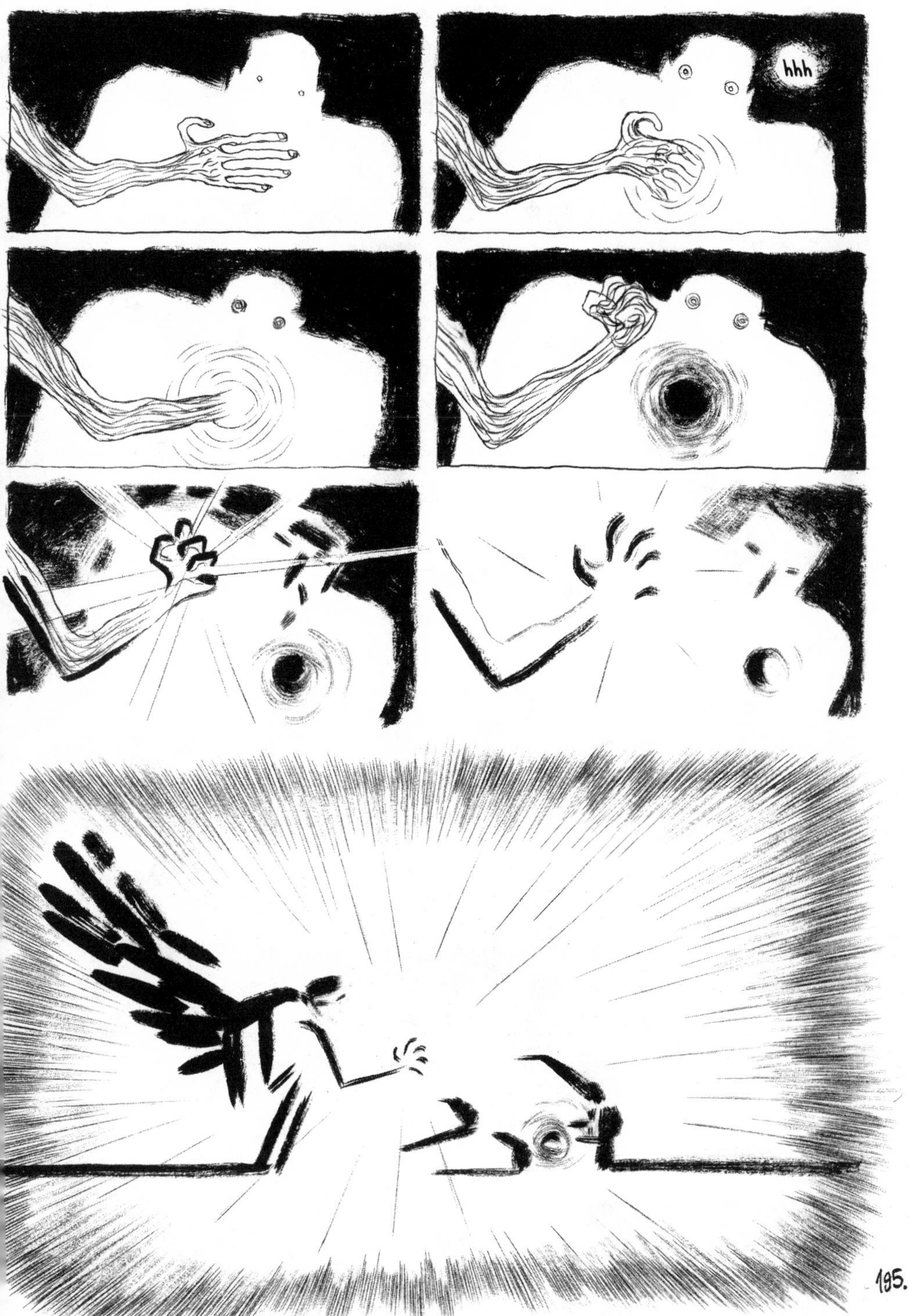
hhh

The old man hadn't lied.

He kept
his word.

With Joachim hidden in my fist...
And my fist in my pocket...
Who could come and take him?

I no longer feared anything.
Or anyone.
Madness.

I was as a golem.

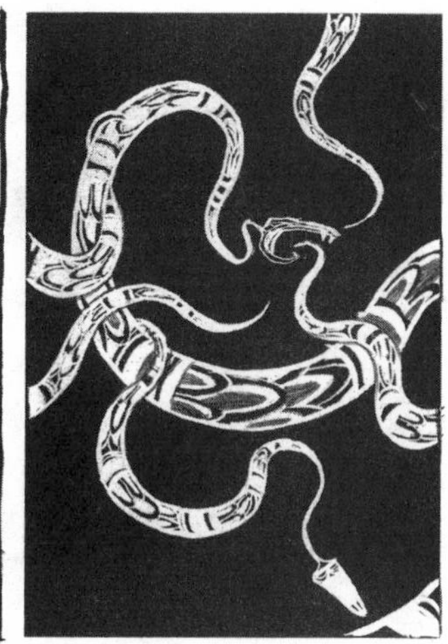

A body driven by defiance.

With wrath where a heart should be, I roamed the plains.

Forded rivers.
Drove back storms.

Douse flames.

Bite dogs.

Break bones.

Bare my teeth.

Kill their masters.

And run...

That's all I know.

How long has it been now?
Days...months, perhaps.

I can remember nothing.
Nothing but this exhaustion.

Endless.

Catch my breath.
And keep moving.
Quickly.
My breath...
A moment.
Just a moment...

Daddy.

Listen to me—please.

I can't live hidden away any longer.

There's no room for me to grow inside your fist.

It's boring here.

Please let me out.

I'm not afraid of the shadows anymore.

Joachim...

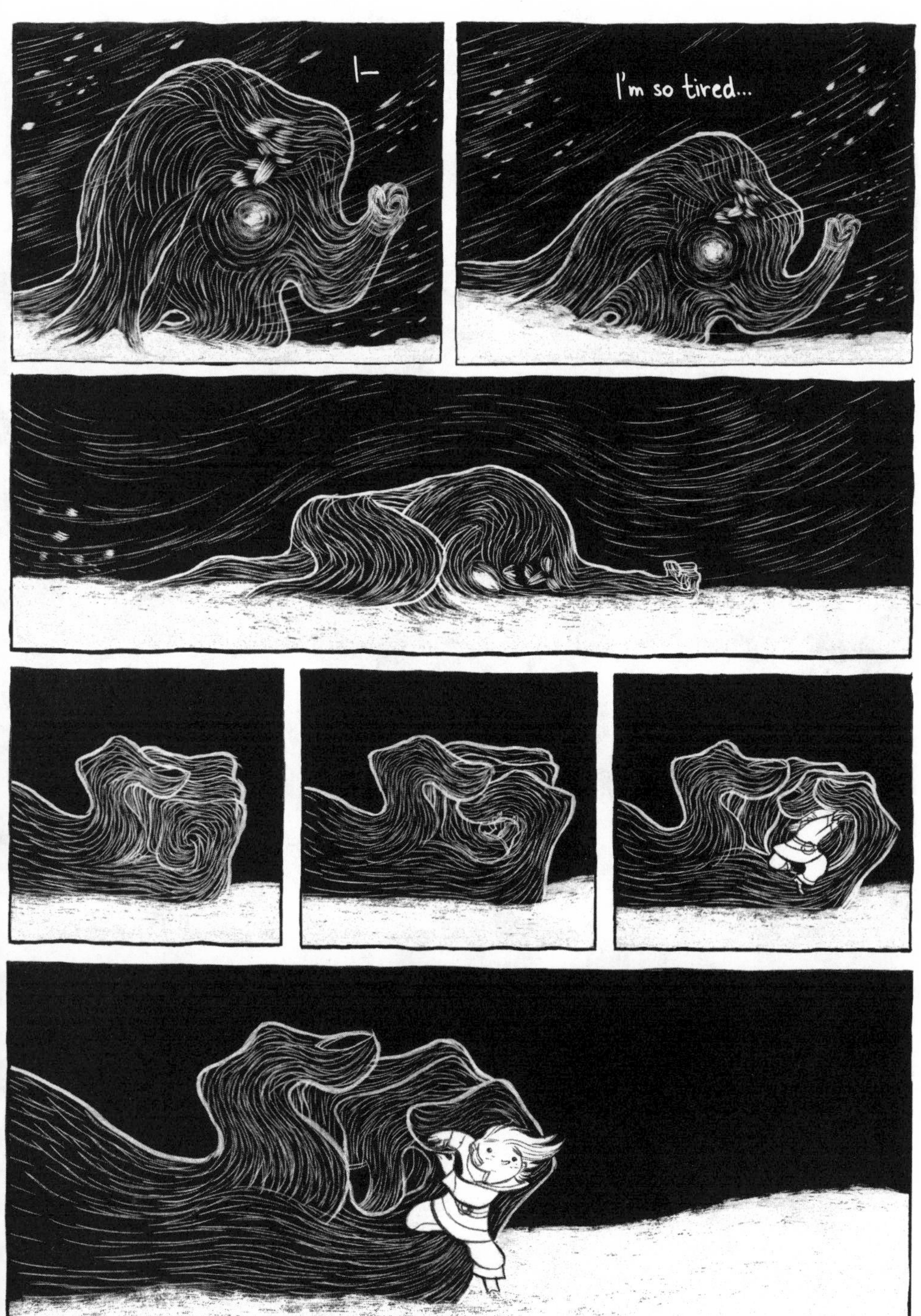
I—
I'm so tired...

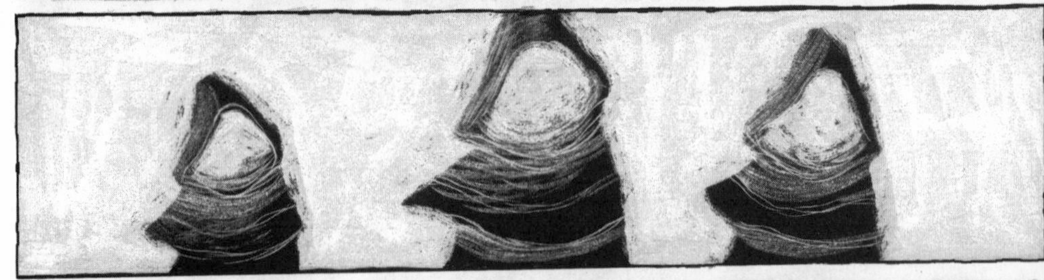

Hello, Joachim.

Are you ready?

It is only life that ends here and now.

Joachim.
You must come with us. Now.

Yes. I understand.

But I'm worried about leaving my dad here like this.

We did not come for him.
Not today.
It's time we were on our way.

That way...

Are we leaving right now?
First, an appointment.

With one who cheats.

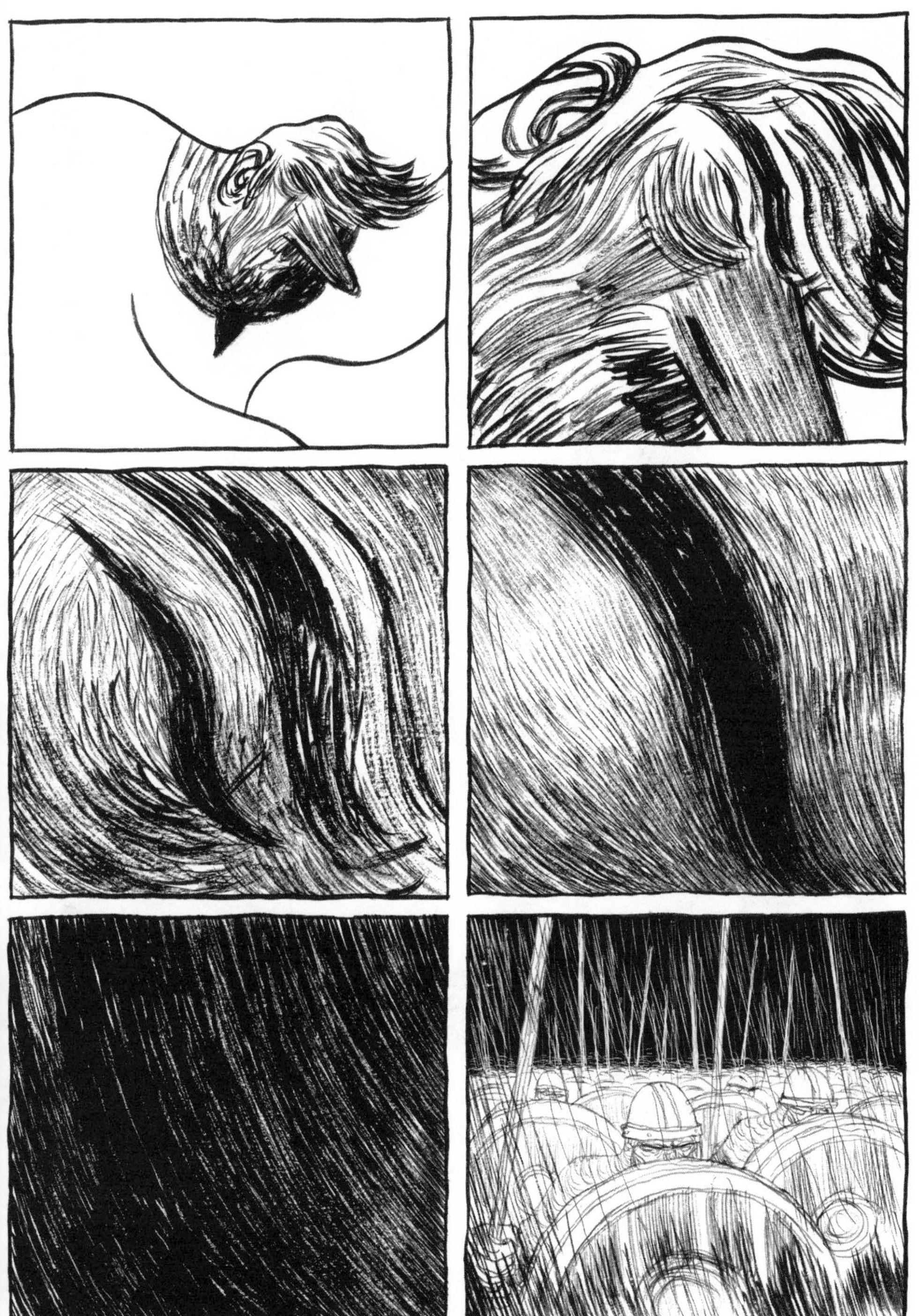

Baste those birds, kitchen boy!
Yes, sir!

And hurry up with the brioche!
scrik scrik

Watch it!

hahaha
hee hee

Pardon
Excuse me
Your Grace
Blah Blah Blah Blah Blah

Back to the lion's den...
Good luck!

...and he fell down!
Ha ha!
hee
hee hee
ha ha ha
ha ha
blah blah blah

blah blah blah
You're getting warmer, my dear!
Look at this!

Does it please you?
hee hee

It's perfect.
This way, my pretty pet!

Whi-iii-ile dancing a jig, my pretty, my pet!!
hee hee

The old baron, in your arms, my pretty, my pet...

Grew tired and his heart gave out, o pretty, o pretty,

The old baron could no longer...
hee hee
What about la Du Montheuil?

That old bag?
Hee hee
Pathetic.

Oh! Monsieur de Rougeret!
Come, my sweet...
A charming little quatrain!

...and I say that little pest doesn't deserve this much consideration...
Your turn, Madame de Charon.

That damned Baron fleeced me!

hahaha
I'm in!
A hundred pistoles!

Have you got it, my friend?
Hmmm...
heh heh

Your Grace, a young lady begs a seat at your table.

A "young lady," you say?
Heavens! What have we here?

"Mademoiselle Aurore"...
Hmm.
Don't know her.

Is she pretty?
Very, Your Grace.

Why didn't you say so before?
ha ha
ha ha
hee hee
Baron, you devi

Well.
What a fortunate coincidence...

De Percy here was just nod-ding off and about to retire.
Me?
Not a
all...

Don't be a fool, de Percy!
The Baron rewards well.
Consider your gambling debts.
So be it.
My dear friends—
It grows late. Madame de Percy surely pines for me.
Permit me my leave.
Baron...
Be off!
Fortune favors the early to bed.
Pascal—
Show the young lady in.

Mademoiselle Aurore!
Come in, my child!
Please, sit down.

We were about to place our bets.
The honor is yours!

My dear Baron, I have a confession to make.
These little monetary bets bore me terribly.
What the devil would you play for?
Then, my dear...

Hmm...
Let's see...
A kiss, perhaps?

A single round of "king's rummy" against you.
Oh!!
What cheek!
Splendid!
Ha ha!

Baron, here's a little lamb just waiting to be fleeced!
Ha ha!
And if I lose?

You will give me an object of my choice.

So be it.
But you shall have to come over and get it yourself.

Incorrigible scoundrel!
He'll make short work of her!
You deprive us of some promising entertainment, dear Baron.
Agreed, dear friend.
But this game no longer concerns you.

Good.
Click

We shall not be disturbed.
It's stifling in here.
Will you give me a moment to freshen up?

But of course.

Psst—
Click

Fortune, it's your game.
You can take my place.
hee hee!
What fun!
That's what bothers me...
This is ridiculous.
I say again, we weren't forced to give ourselves up to this farce.
What a killjoy!
Ssh! Enough talk!
Go on!
And don't forget, Silkie needs to replace you when the round's over.
At last!
I thought you'd been kid-napped by prowling brigands!
Ha ha!
Come now, Baron...
You know ho
the saying goes:

"One must know how to make one's enemies wait."
heh heh
flick
fleck
flick
fleck
Let the games begin.
The honor is yours.
Draw.
Pass.
sniff

Run of three.
Pass.
sniff
sniff
Draw.
Pass.
Heh heh...three of a kind.
Your turn, my pet.
Hmm...
Ahem—
Well.
Voilà.

Royal run!

Tee hee!

My word!
I don't know how you do it, but you cheat better than I do!
Bravo.
Hic!
Excuse me.

Hic!
The wine, no doubt...

I'm not used—
Hic!

to—
Hic!

...
Heavens above!
Your hair!
What the—
My God!
Hic!
Please excuse me, I must—
Not so fast!
You can't leave without explaining this feat!
How dare you—!
Unhand me immediately.
Aaah!
Wham

Aarrgh!!
Cursed woman!

Witchcraft doesn't impress me!

Now answer me!
Who are you?
What do you want?
Hic!
What do you think?

That's it!
This joke's gone far enough!

You'd have stopped at nothing to delay us, wouldn't you?
Is your life so very precious?

It's worth all the gold in the world!
You know that quite well.

You cheated and stole from a man.
He cheated himself.
His life belongs to me now!

If you want it—
You have to come and get it!

hahahaha

KRAASH

Hmph!
What a waste of time!
Hic!

KRACK KRICK

Raargh!

unhhh

Hic!
Whatever pos-sessed you to try that wine?

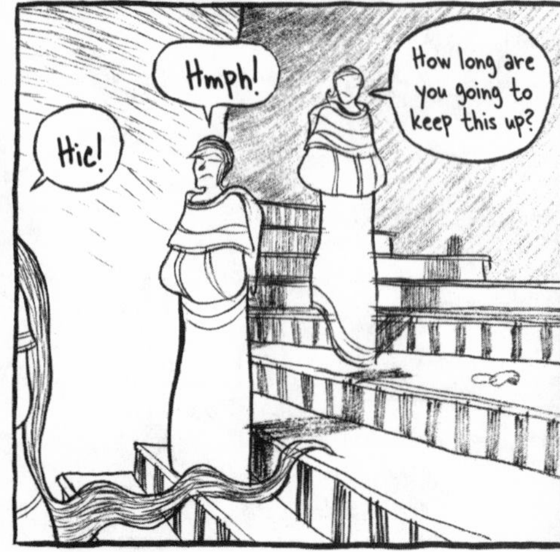
Hmph!
Hic!
How long are you going to keep this up?

huff
huff

screee

WHAM

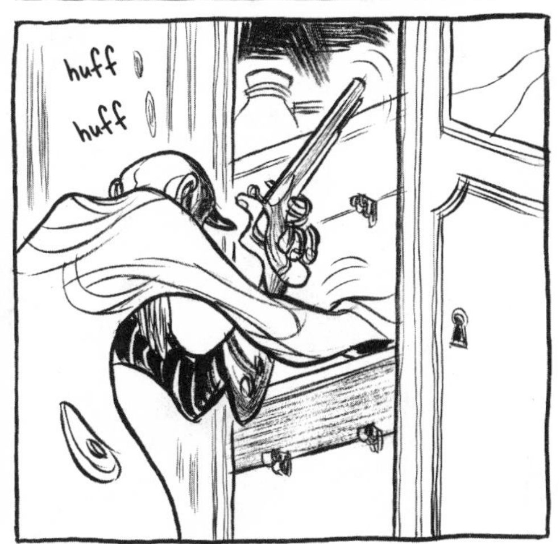
huff
huff

tap
tap
tap
tap
tap
tap

tap
tap
Hie!
tap
tap
tap tap

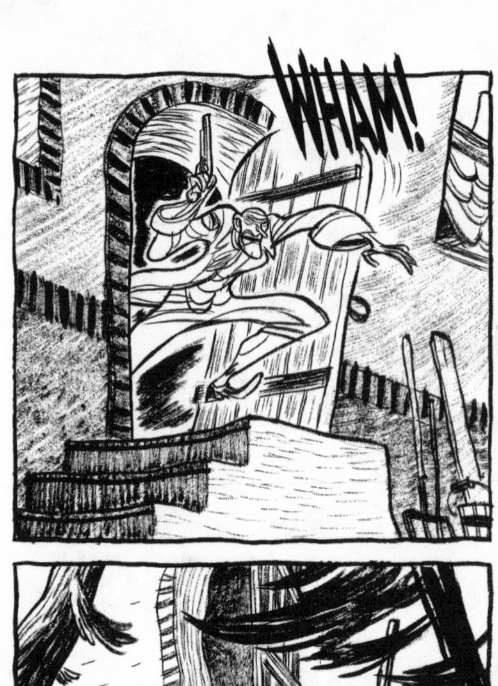
WHAM!

hhh
hhh

huff
huff

huff
huff

hhh
hhh

Raaaa!

WHAM

Watch out!!
hhh

Tap
Tap
Tap

Baron.
Your time is well beyond its end.

You know this.

You cannot usurp another's life with impunity.

snip

You had thought
to escape yourself.
In reality...
...you only hastened toward your fate.

Henceforth...

...you shall have all eternity...

...to pay the price for this stolen life.

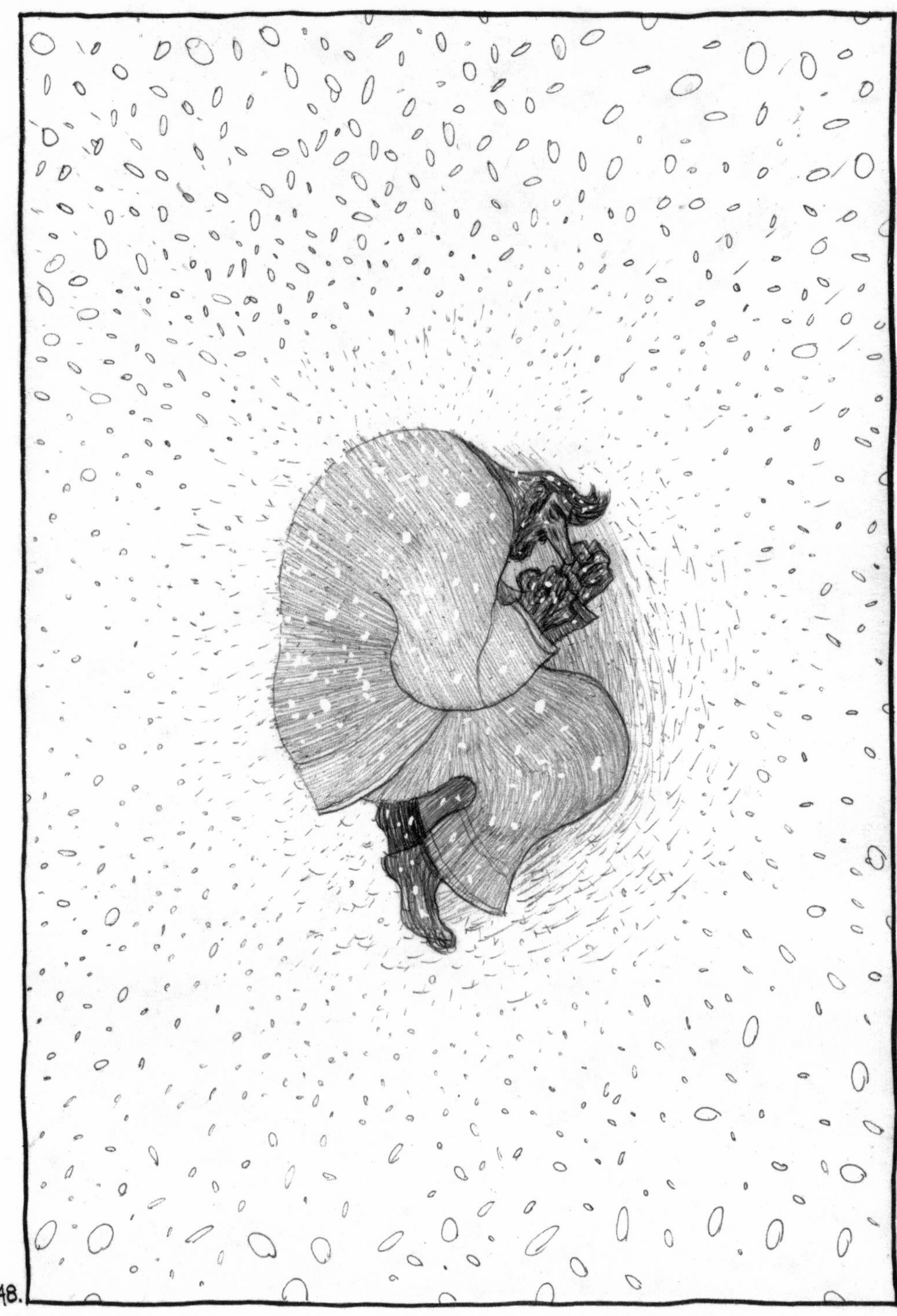

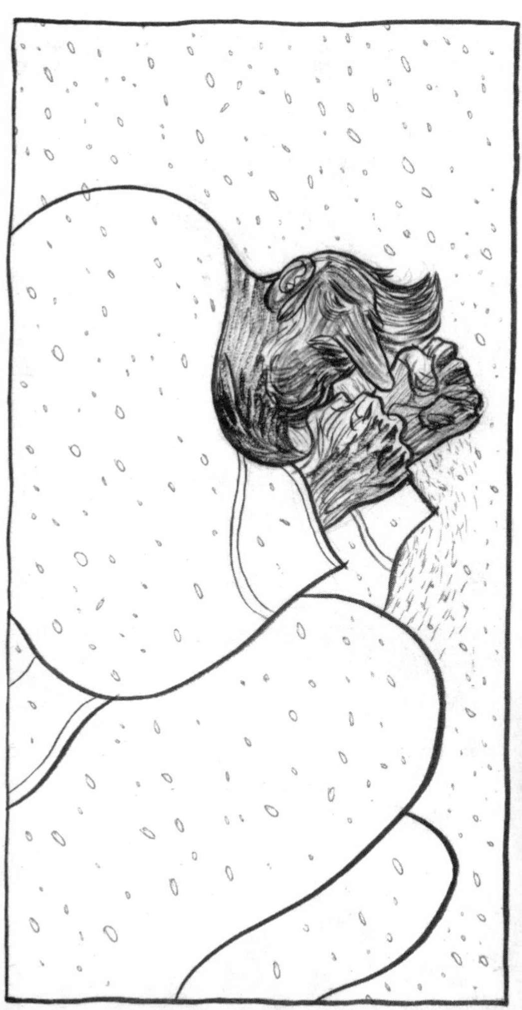

Joachim...

I thought you'd never come back!
What a funny idea.
There remains one last task before us.

We do not have the power to restore the breath of life to your father's heart.

Only you can do so, before leaving.

Thank you.

Do not thank us.
We decide nothing.
It is so.
When his day comes...
...we shall return for your father.

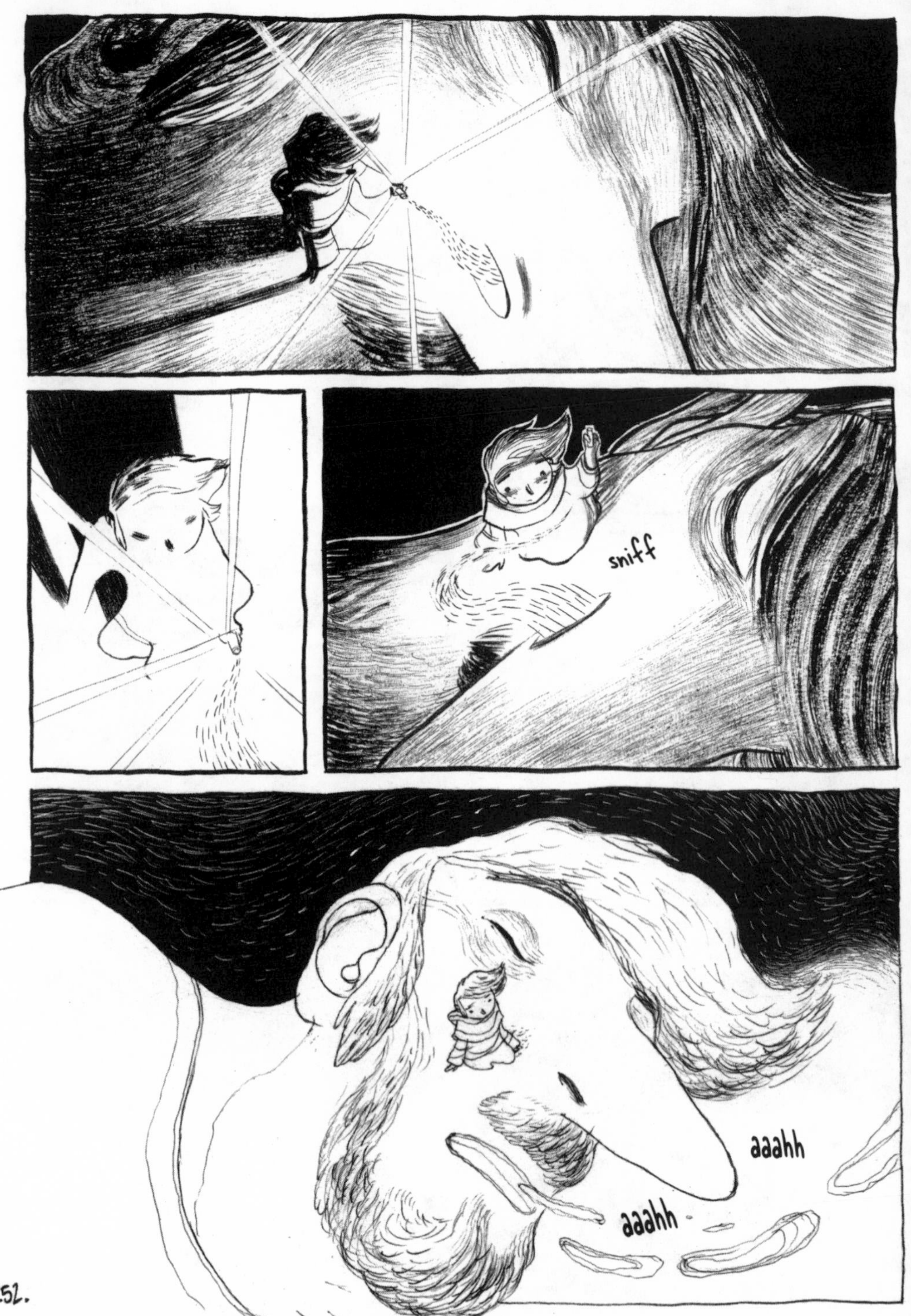
sniff
aaahh
aaahh

aaahh
aaahh

We must go.
Joachim...

All right.

Goodbye, Dad.

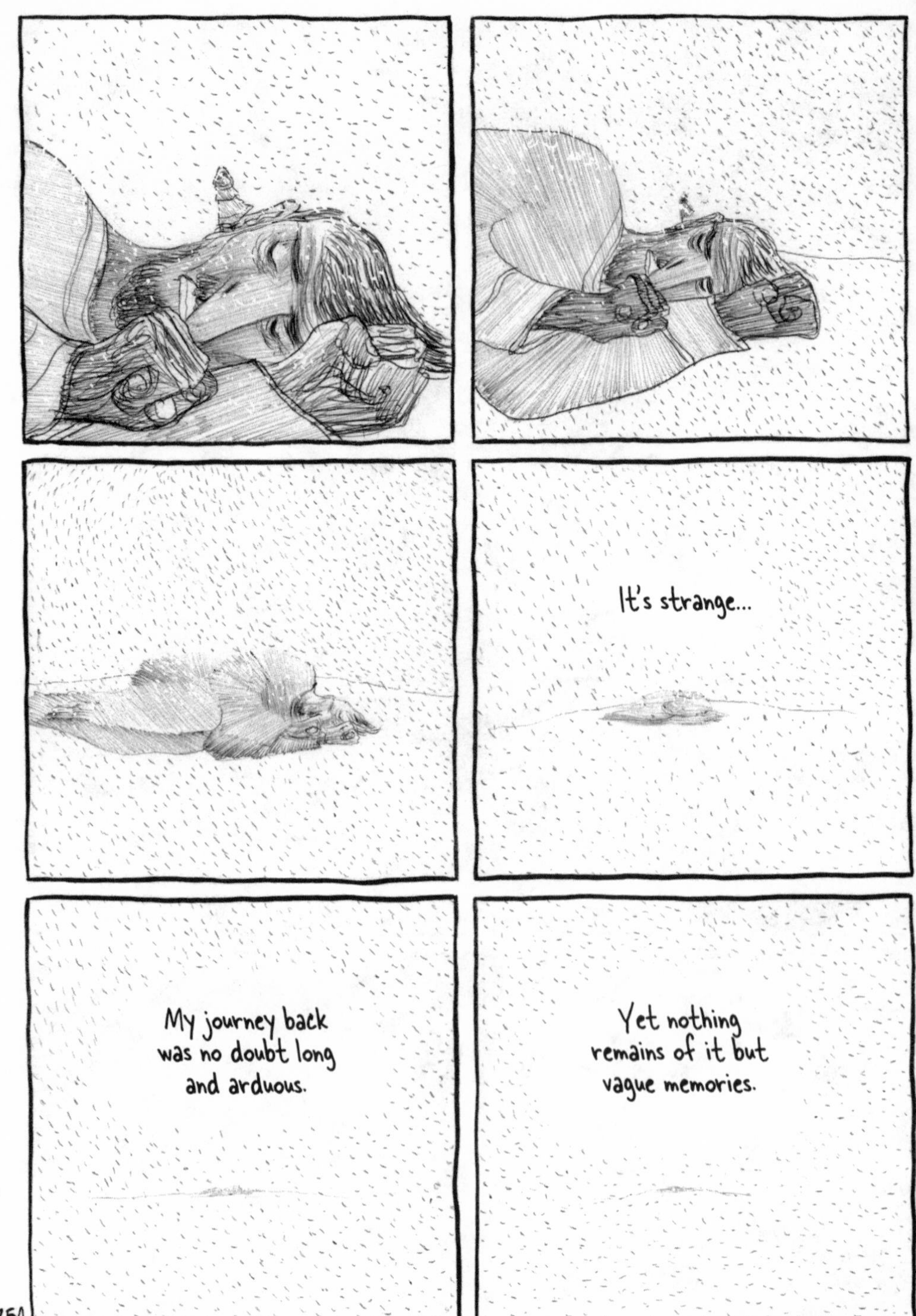
It's strange...
My journey back was no doubt long and arduous.
Yet nothing remains of it but vague memories.

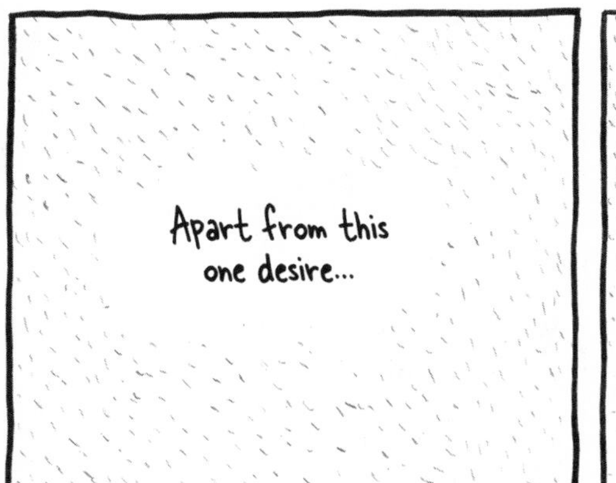
Apart from this
one desire...

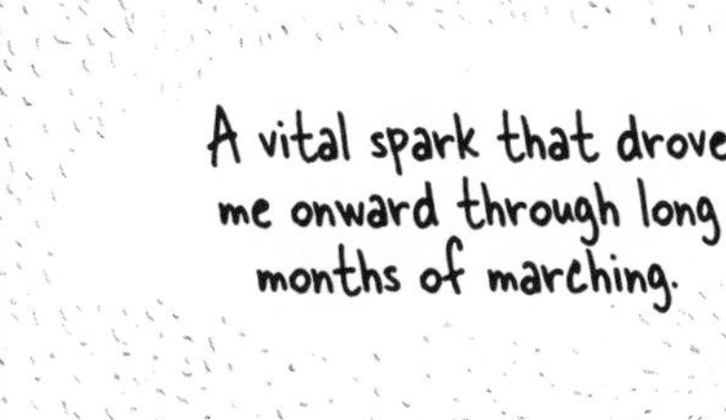
A vital spark that drove
me onward through long
months of marching.

Seeing Lise
once more.

WHAM

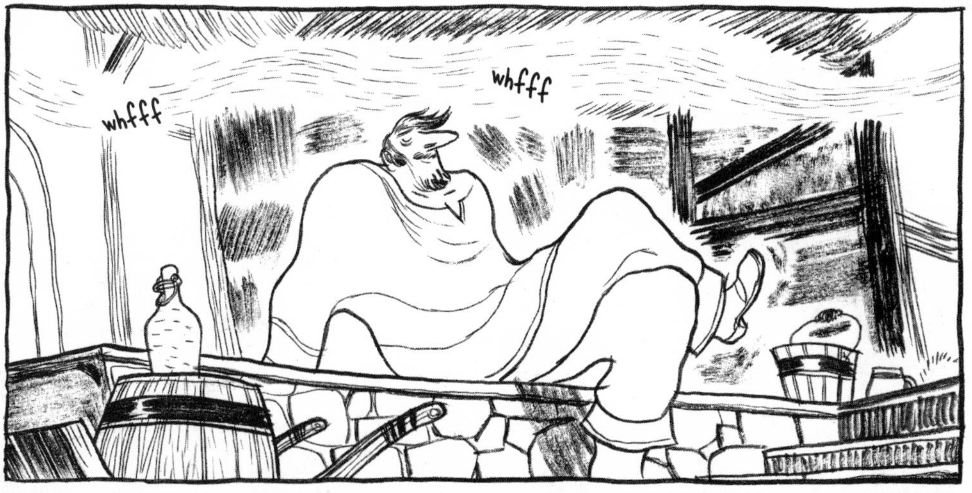
whfff
whfff

whfff

Daddy!

Daddieeee!
Daddieeee!
ha ha
We found wild strawberries!
Yay!
Fabulous!
Look!
Mommy says you can't eat them because foxes pee on them!
And pee makes you sick!
Hmm...hmmm...
In that case...
We haven't any choice.
We'll have to try one and see.

Ewww!
slurtch
slurp
Well? Are they okay?
Yum...delici—
AAARGH!
Ha ha!
Hee hee!
Arrrggh! Help!!
This basket is extremely heavy—
—but I'll just muddle on through!
C'mon, Daddy!
Try another pee berry!
Don't mind me!
Ha ha ha...No, I think your mother needs my help.

So, how was it?
peck
Good! The woods are beautiful right now.

You should've seen it.
Your daughters were really quite good at finding strawberries.
Shall we go for a picnic tomorrow?

Yes, if you want.

I know...
Me too...

Hee hee hee—

Look at them...

Mommieee!

Do chickens really like them?

Don't you believe me?

Yay!

ha ha ha

See?

I told you so.

bock bock bock

We could even go swimming after the picnic, right?

Not so fast! You'll eat them all!

ha ha ha